INTRODUCTION
THE REIGN BEGINS

Ninety feet. That's all that separated the Royals from a possible World Series championship in 2014. It would have been the franchise's first title since 1985. Instead, Alex Gordon, who represented the game's tying run, was left stranded at third base in the ninth inning of Game 7 as the San Francisco Giants celebrated their third title in five years.

As difficult as those last 90 feet were for Kansas City to overcome, the club made an even longer journey, one of the 162-game variety, look quite easy. In 2015, spurred on by a renewed purpose, the Royals led their division wire-to-wire on their way to assembling the American League's best record.

The postseason, however, was a different story. The team barely held off an upstart Houston Astros team in an ALDS that went the full five games. In the American League Championship Series, the Royals were able to subdue the Toronto Blue Jays' bats just enough to clinch their second consecutive World Series berth.

The Fall Classic pitted Kansas City against a young and extremely talented New York Mets squad, which sported a stable of hard-throwing arms in its starting rotation. Taking the world title in five games, the Royals made their victory look predestined, executing perfectly on offense, defense and the mound to clinch a title exactly 30 years after their last.

FORMER ROYALS GREAT GEORGE BRETT (OPPOSITE, BOTTOM) THREW OUT THE CEREMONIAL FIRST PITCH BEFORE EDINSON VOLQUEZ (OPPOSITE, TOP RIGHT) TOOK THE MOUND IN GAME 1. THE ROYALS AND THEIR FANS REVELED IN THEIR 5-4 VICTORY, SPARKED BY ALCIDES ESCOBAR'S INSIDE-THE-PARK HOME RUN.

BEN ZOBRIST, SALVADOR PEREZ (OPPOSITE, TOP LEFT AND RIGHT) AND MIKE MOUSTAKAS (LEFT) CAME PREPARED FOR GAME 2, BUT THEIR WORK IN THE FIELD WAS MADE EASY THANKS TO A DOMINANT PERFORMANCE FROM JOHNNY CUETO (ABOVE). THE RIGHT-HANDER WITH A FUNKY DELIVERY BECAME THE FIRST AMERICAN LEAGUE PITCHER TO THROW A COMPLETE GAME IN THE WORLD SERIES SINCE 1991. HE WAS ASSISTED BY AN OFFENSE THAT "KEPT THE LINE MOVIN'," SCORING FOUR RUNS ON FIVE HITS IN A FATEFUL FIFTH INNING. THE COMBINATION PROVED TOO MUCH FOR THE METS TO HANDLE, AS THE ROYALS NOTCHED THEIR SECOND STRAIGHT HOME VICTORY.

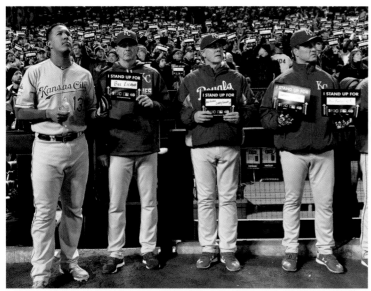

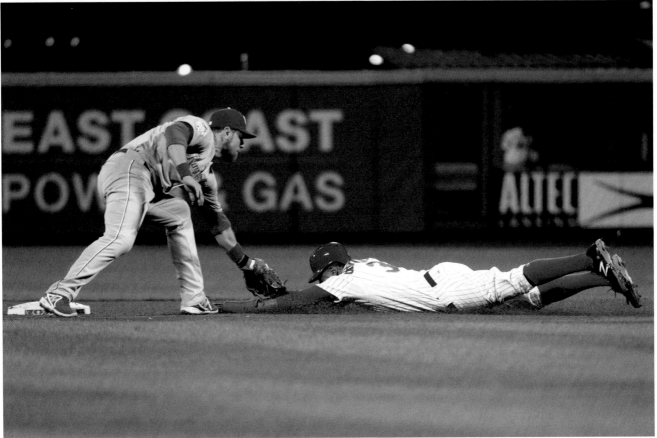

KANSAS CITY PAUSED TO STAND UP TO CANCER IN GAME 3 (OPPOSITE, TOP LEFT). THE METS PROVED IN THAT CONTEST THAT THEY WEREN'T OUT YET, DESPITE EFFORTS BY ALEX GORDON (OPPOSITE, TOP RIGHT) AND ALEX RIOS (OPPOSITE, BOTTOM). THE ROYALS' TENACITY WAS ON DISPLAY IN GAME 4, WITH STELLAR PERFORMANCES BY MIKE MOUSTAKAS (TOP, LEFT), LORENZO CAIN (TOP, RIGHT) AND BEN ZOBRIST (TAGGING OUT GRANDERSON).

THE KANSAS CITY ROYALS CELEBRATED
THEIR WORLD SERIES CHAMPIONSHIP.
JOHNNY CUETO (OPPOSITE, TOP) HOISTED
THE COMMISSIONER'S TROPHY.
ACTOR PAUL RUDD (OPPOSITE, BOTTOM)
JOINEDo IN THE FESTIVITIES.

KAUFFMAN STADIUM

The only true ballpark built during the multipurpose stadium era of the '60s and '70s, Kauffman Stadium opened in 1973, and its debut coincided with the emergence of a dynamic young Kansas City team. Speedsters and gap hitters ran wild on the park's artificial turf that year, and the Royals made the playoffs seven times from 1976–85.

With its terrific sightlines and signature lighted fountains, Kauffman Stadium is a masterpiece. Originally called Royals Stadium, the ballpark was renamed in 1993 after the team's founding owner, Ewing M. Kauffman, and one of only two current American League stadiums named after an individual.

Kansas City's first home, Municipal Stadium, was a chameleon of a ballpark during its 50-year lifespan, hosting four storied baseball franchises, as well as the NFL's Kansas City Chiefs, who now have a home of their own just across the parking lot from The K. Opened in 1923 as the home of the Minor League Kansas City Blues and the Negro Leagues' Monarchs, it was the first stadium in the world to regularly host night games, and the site of many of legendary pitcher Satchel Paige's finest moments.

Kauffman, which received a $250-million facelift in 2009, still offers one of baseball's great experiences. The K celebrated its 40th anniversary two years ago, and has hosted more than 74 million fans since its opening. This year, the stadium welcomed the World Series for the second consecutive season and the fourth time overall.

ALTHOUGH IT IS THE FOURTH-OLDEST BALLPARK IN THE JUNIOR CIRCUIT, KAUFFMAN STADIUM REMAINS ONE OF THE MOST PICTURESQUE, HIGHLIGHTED BY ITS SIGNATURE OUTFIELD FOUNTAINS AND CROWN VISION SCOREBOARD.

17

2015: SEASON IN REVIEW

"In baseball, you don't know nothing," late Hall of Famer Yogi Berra once said, encapsulating the game in the succinct yet profound manner that only he could. Seasons come and go, but what happens on the diamond each year is bound to be unique and exciting. And this year was no different, as fans were lucky enough to witness a plethora of milestones and oddities.

Between Games 1 and 162, youngsters reached new heights and veterans further cemented their legacies. Long home runs dazzled fans, while dominant pitching performances took their breath away. Once-in-a-lifetime matchups and historic debuts filled ballparks across the country. Yet through it all, there remained a common thread: Baseball in 2015 proved just as unpredictable as ever.

FINAL 2015 STANDINGS

AMERICAN LEAGUE

EAST	W	L	GB
y Toronto	93	69	–
w New York	87	75	6
Baltimore	81	81	12
Tampa Bay	80	82	13
Boston	78	84	15

CENTRAL	W	L	GB
y Kansas City	95	67	–
Minnesota	83	79	12
Cleveland	81	80	13.5
Chicago	76	86	19
Detroit	74	87	20.5

WEST	W	L	GB
y Texas	88	74	–
w Houston	86	76	2
Los Angeles	85	77	3
Seattle	76	86	12
Oakland	68	94	20

NATIONAL LEAGUE

EAST	W	L	GB
y New York	90	72	–
Washington	83	79	7
Miami	71	91	19
Atlanta	67	95	23
Philadelphia	63	99	27

CENTRAL	W	L	GB
y St. Louis	100	62	–
w Pittsburgh	98	64	2
w Chicago	97	65	3
Milwaukee	68	94	32
Cincinnati	64	98	36

WEST	W	L	GB
y Los Angeles	92	70	–
San Francisco	84	78	8
Arizona	79	83	13
San Diego	74	88	18
Colorado	68	94	24

y Division winner; w Wild Card

CATEGORY LEADERS

AMERICAN LEAGUE

Batting Average	Miguel Cabrera, Detroit	.338
Hits	Jose Altuve, Houston	200
Home Runs	Chris Davis, Baltimore	47
RBI	Josh Donaldson, Toronto	123
Stolen Bases	Jose Altuve, Houston	38
Wins	Dallas Keuchel, Houston	20
ERA	David Price, Detroit/Toronto	2.45
Strikeouts	Chris Sale, Chicago	274
Saves	Brad Boxberger, Tampa Bay	41

NATIONAL LEAGUE

Batting Average	Dee Gordon, Miami	.333
Hits	Dee Gordon, Miami	205
Home Runs	Nolan Arenado, Colorado Bryce Harper, Washington	42
RBI	Nolan Arenado, Colorado	130
Stolen Bases	Dee Gordon, Miami	58
Wins	Jake Arrieta, Chicago	22
ERA	Zack Greinke, Los Angeles	1.66
Strikeouts	Clayton Kershaw, Los Angeles	301
Saves	Mark Melancon, Pittsburgh	51

A WILD FINISH

With a Wild Card spot and a division still up for grabs as the calendar flipped to October, some teams narrowly missed out on their postseason dreams. The American League West experienced the greatest flurry of action in the season's closing days, as the Angels, Rangers and Astros all vied for the division crown, with three games separating the trio in the final week and an Angels–Rangers showdown looming. Raising the stakes of the division race was the knowledge that the Yankees had claimed the first AL Wild Card spot, leaving only one up for grabs.

Houston beat the Diamondbacks two out of three games in Arizona to close the season, while the Angels and Rangers split the first two games of their series. Even on the season's final day, all three clubs still had the chance to either win the division or secure the Wild Card spot. In the end, it was Texas, fueled by clutch hits from veteran slugger Adrian Beltre and a Cole Hamels complete game, that toppled L.A. to take the division crown. And with the Angels' loss, the Astros squeezed into the second Wild Card opening. They would quickly capitalize on the opportunity, as they shut out New York in the AL Wild Card Game to advance to a Division Series showdown against Kansas City.

APRIL

MOOSE CROSSING

On a mission to prove that last year was no fluke, the defending AL champion Royals sizzled out of the gate, securing seven straight wins to open the 2015 campaign. Third baseman **Mike Moustakas** knocked two hits and worked a walk to help Kansas City win its seventh game in a row, and he was largely influential to the club's impressive start overall. During the season's first month, Moose tallied 11 multi-hit games and posted a robust .356/.420/.522 slash line while scoring 19 runs. More importantly, the 27-year-old parlayed the hot start into a banner year at the plate; the first-time All-Star set career-high marks in home runs, RBI, runs scored, hits and average.

OPEN AND SHUT CASE

Several aces, including **David Price**, dominated during Opening Night and Day, as the Cardinals, Tigers, Red Sox, Astros, A's and Rockies started the season off right with a record-setting six shutouts.

TRIPLE THREAT

Speedy Royals outfielder **Paulo Orlando** began his Big League career with a bang; on April 12, he legged out his third straight triple to become the first player since 1900 to record three-baggers for his first three hits.

MIGHTY MIKE

Mike Trout launched two homers against the Houston Astros on April 17 to become the youngest player in MLB history with 100 home runs and 100 stolen bases. The outfielder was 23 years and 253 days old at the time, edging out Alex Rodriguez's mark by a mere 56 days.

MAY

ERIC THE GREAT

Fan favorite **Eric Hosmer** helped lead the Royals to the Fall Classic last season, and the first baseman picked up right where he left off in 2015. On May 1, Hosmer went 3 for 4 with two runs scored to start the month with a bang, and it was a sign of things to come. Hosmer would bat .296 in May with 16 RBI and 18 runs scored, forging a formidable middle of the order along with Mike Moustakas and Lorenzo Cain. The former first-round pick took another leap forward at the plate this season, besting both 90 RBI and 90 runs scored for the first time in his career.

NO. 660

Alex Rodriguez collected his 660th home run on May 1, tying Hall of Famer Willie Mays for fourth place on the all-time list. The longtime Yankee would pass Mays just six days later in a game against the Orioles.

LOCKED IN

Cardinals outfielder **Matt Holliday** set an NL record on May 27 by reaching base safely in each of the season's first 43 games. Fittingly, Holliday broke the long-standing mark (42) set by former teammate Albert Pujols on his quest, which ended after 45 games.

FRESHMAN FIREPOWER

Also on May 27, sensational freshman **Kris Bryant** blasted a pitch off the new video board in left field at Wrigley. The 23-year-old more than lived up to his No. 1 prospect status, as he set a Cubs rookie record for home runs and plated 99 runs with a .369 OBP in just his first Major League season.

JUNE

'PEN-ULTIMATE

On June 2, **Wade Davis** gave up his first run in 22 innings and watched his ERA skyrocket — all the way up to 0.39. All jokes aside, Davis was utterly dominant out of the 'pen once again in 2015. By the end of the month, his ERA was back down to 0.27, and he would finish the season with an otherworldly 0.94 mark to lead all Royals relievers. The hurler struck out more than 10 batters per nine innings with a 0.79 WHIP, and his eight wins were tied for fourth most on the team. Davis also notched a career-high 17 saves after taking over the closer's role from Greg Holland, who needed season-ending Tommy John surgery late in the year.

DUAL THREAT
On June 5, baseball fans got to witness a rare feat: the debut of a switch-pitcher. **Pat Venditte** took the mound for the Oakland A's and threw both left- and right-handed for two innings total against the Boston Red Sox.

GENERATIONAL GREATS
When **Prince Fielder** notched his 300th career longball on June 26 against the Blue Jays, he joined exclusive company; Prince and his father, Cecil, became the second father-son duo in Major League history (after Bobby and Barry Bonds) to each notch more than 300 home runs. The Rangers first baseman enjoyed a resurgent season after missing most of 2014 with neck surgery, leading his team in average, RBI and on-base percentage.

HITTING HURLER
On June 28, **Steven Matz** not only picked up his first career win, but also became the first pitcher in history to drive in four or more runs in his Major League debut.

JULY

CENTER OF IT ALL

While **Lorenzo Cain** dazzled in center field throughout the 2014 campaign, the outfielder used the next season to prove that he could also dominate at the plate. The 31-day span from July's start to end proved to be a microcosm of Cain's season. The speedy 29-year-old launched five homers, a number that matched his 2014 *total*, while batting .367 and scoring 22 runs. That surge in power continued for the rest of the year as Cain improved across the board offensively, shattering his career-high mark in home runs by nine, RBI by 19 and runs scored by 46.

WHO'S AT FIRST?

Designated hitter **David Ortiz** made a rare start at first base on July 5 and incidentally entered the franchise record books: For the first time in Boston's 17,867-game history, the home team's first baseman did not record a putout.

KINGS OF THE QUEEN CITY

The 2015 All-Star Game and Home Run Derby at Great American Ball Park were part of a fitting showcase for the hometown boys. Reds third baseman **Todd Frazier** slugged 15 homers in just four minutes and 30 seconds to win the Derby crown, while fireballer Aroldis Chapman entered the Midsummer Classic in the ninth and promptly struck out the side on 14 pitches to the delight of the crowd.

ZACK ATTACK

On July 26, **Zack Greinke** brought a scoreless innings streak into his seventh straight start. His impressive run finished at 45.2 innings, though, when Mets pitcher Jacob deGrom earned an RBI on a fielder's choice. The streak was the longest since 1988 and ended 13.1 innings shy of the all-time mark set by another Dodgers hurler, Orel Hershiser.

AUGUST

SUMMER HEAT

On Aug. 27, **Yordano Ventura** authored perhaps his most dominant performance of the season, as he struck out 11 batters and gave up just two hits in six scoreless innings against the Baltimore Orioles. The outing netted him his fourth win of the month in six starts, and it's this impressive upside that has Kansas City fans' mouths watering. Through ups and downs, including a stint in the Minors this season, Ventura has repeatedly shown that he has an impressive arsenal, and his fastball, which averages over 95 miles per hour, is the fastest in the Majors among starting pitchers.

SAVE THE DATE
In early August, 42-year-old **LaTroy Hawkins** joined the Blue Jays, his 11th MLB club. And with a scoreless ninth on Aug. 5, the veteran pitcher became the 13th player in history to record a save against every Big League team.

HOME SWEET HOME
On Aug. 11, all 15 home teams — including **Dee Gordon**'s Marlins, who walked off at Marlins Park in the 10th inning against Boston — won for the first time in baseball history. According to Elias Sports Bureau, the closest that home teams had previously come to this feat was 12 wins on May 23, 1914.

BROTHERLY LOVE?
On Aug. 22, **Gerrit Cole** picked up a seemingly routine win with seven innings of one-run ball. Yet this W was particularly personal, as the Pirates' ace struck out his soon-to-be brother-in-law, Brandon Crawford, twice during the contest.

SEPTEMBER/OCTOBER

A ROYAL RETURN

September brought with it the return of one of Kansas City's star players, as **Alex Gordon** made his way back to the Royals' lineup on the first day of the month. The left fielder had been on the disabled list since July 8, when he suffered a groin strain while attempting to track down a fly ball. After getting on base at an impressive .394 clip in the first three-and-a-half months of the season, Gordon also finished the campaign strong upon his return, collecting a hit in nine of his last 10 games to help Kansas City secure the American League's top record.

PUT ME IN, COACH

On Sept. 15, the Colorado Rockies and Los Angeles Dodgers faced off in an intra-division matchup that featured the most players (58) and pitchers (24) ever used in a single game. Third baseman **Nolan Arenado** launched his 39th longball of the season in the 16th inning to finally end the standoff.

MAD MAX

On Oct. 3, **Max Scherzer** distinguished himself as just the sixth player in history to throw two no-hitters in a season. After hurling a near-perfecto in June, the Nats' ace whiffed 17 Mets, tying Nolan Ryan for the most K's in a no-no while allowing only one batter to reach base on an error.

A WIN-WIN FOR THE BIG APPLE

The **Yankees** notched a historic win on Oct. 1, as they not only secured a Wild Card berth but also collected their 10,000th franchise victory. New York ranks eighth overall in wins among MLB clubs but boasts the best winning percentage.

IN BOTH THE JUNIOR AND SENIOR CIRCUITS, THE CY YOUNG RACE WAS TIGHT FROM START TO FINISH. WORTHY CANDIDATES, LIKE (CLOCKWISE FROM FAR LEFT) ARRIETA, PRICE, KEUCHEL, KERSHAW AND GREINKE, EACH PROVED THEIR METTLE ON THE MOUND TIME AND TIME AGAIN.

ARMS RACE

Oftentimes, the Cy Young Award seems to be locked up well before the season finishes. In 2014, for instance, Clayton Kershaw's mastery on the mound was so profound that he was the only logical choice for the NL award. But this year, the race was as tight as ever.

In the Junior Circuit, two pitchers stood out among the pack. Toronto's David Price arrived north of the border at the trade deadline and injected new life into a team that ended a 21-year playoff drought. Price led the AL in ERA while placing fourth with 225 K's. Further south, Houston's Dallas Keuchel compiled an AL-best WHIP and a 15-0 record at home, a Major League–best mark. The Astros' ground ball specialist added to an already stellar campaign by hurling six shutout innings to propel Houston over the Yankees in the AL Wild Card Game.

The Senior Circuit flaunted the top two pitchers by ERA this season, Zack Greinke and Jake Arrieta. Greinke's mark never topped 2.00 this season, he boasted the Majors' best winning percentage and he allowed one run or fewer in 21 starts, a feat achieved just five other times in history. Arrieta, on the other hand, notched 22 wins, including a no-hitter, and finished the season by allowing just four earned runs from Aug. 4 through Oct. 2. He then fired a shutout in the NL Wild Card Game to send Chicago to the NLDS.

The sheer dominance of each pitcher is reminiscent of the 1985 campaign, the last in which two pitchers boasted sub-2.00 ERAs. And let's not forget a final dark horse candidate: perennial, and reigning, Cy Young Award winner Clayton Kershaw. Last year's NL MVP enjoyed another remarkable season, posting a 2.13 ERA and 0.88 WHIP while striking out 301 batters, the highest mark since 2002 and the most by a Dodgers moundsman since Sandy Koufax. Each of these five hurlers' efforts were integral in strong-arming their teams into the postseason.

AMERICAN LEAGUE DIVISION SERIES

GAME 1, OCTOBER 8
HOUSTON 5, KANSAS CITY 2

After knocking off the New York Yankees in the AL Wild Card Game, the Houston Astros were primed to face the reigning American League champion Kansas City Royals in the Division Series. The Astros, though, wasted no time proving they would be a tough out. In front of a raucous Kauffman Stadium crowd, Houston got on the board in the top of the first inning in Game 1 via RBI groundouts from Colby Rasmus and Evan Gattis. Jose Altuve added an RBI single in the second inning, providing starter Collin McHugh with a three-run advantage, and ultimately all the run support he would need to prevail.

Designated hitter Kendrys Morales drilled two solo home runs off McHugh to account for the Royals' offense. But those proved to be the only blemishes of the night for the 28-year-old starter, who pitched six strong innings in his postseason debut, which included a 49-minute rain delay following the second inning.

George Springer and Rasmus knocked solo home runs in the fifth and eighth innings, respectively, to add some insurance and secure a 5-2, opening game victory on the road for the Astros.

	1	2	3	4	5	6	7	8	9	R	H	E
HOUSTON	2	1	0	0	1	0	0	1	0	5	11	0
KANSAS CITY	0	1	0	1	0	0	0	0	0	2	6	0

WP: McHugh **LP:** Ventura **SV:** Gregerson
HR: HOU: Springer, Rasmus KC: Morales (2)

RASMUS WAS RESPONSIBLE FOR TWO OF THE ASTROS' FIVE RUNS IN THEIR GAME 1 VICTORY AND ADDED A STOLEN BASE, AS WELL.

"You take it day by day. It's a five-game series. The first team to win three is going to be the winner. It's not a death sentence to lose Game 1."

Royals Manager Ned Yost

GAME 2, OCTOBER 9
KANSAS CITY 5, HOUSTON 4

Just as in the series opener, Houston struck early in Game 2. Once again, Colby Rasmus was right in the middle of the action for the Astros. The outfielder doubled home George Springer in the first before drilling his third home run of the postseason in the third inning to stake Houston to a three-run lead.

But this time, Kansas City would strike back. Down by two runs in the sixth, the Royals would finally summon the never-say-die attitude that defined their magical 2014 postseason. Eric Hosmer followed a Lorenzo Cain double with an RBI single to pull the Royals within one. Two batters later, Salvador Perez drew a bases-loaded walk that forced in Hosmer to tie the game.

The next inning, Alcides Escobar knocked a leadoff triple and Ben Zobrist drove him home, handing a 5-4 lead off to Kansas City's vaunted bullpen.

Ryan Madson and Wade Davis each pitched a scoreless inning of relief to nail down the win and even the ALDS at a game apiece before the series shifted to Houston.

	1	2	3	4	5	6	7	8	9	R	H	E
HOUSTON	1	2	1	0	0	0	0	0	0	4	8	0
KANSAS CITY	0	1	1	0	0	2	1	0	X	5	11	0

WP: Herrera **LP:** Harris **SV:** Davis
HR: KC: Perez HOU: Rasmus

DAVIS CAME ON IN RELIEF OF STARTER JOHNNY CUETO IN GAME 2, AND HE AUTHORED A SCORELESS NINTH WITH ONE K TO LOCK DOWN THE WIN.

HOSMER (LEFT) COLLECTED AN RBI BASE KNOCK AND CAME AROUND TO SCORE, WHILE ZOBRIST DROVE IN THE GAME WINNER AS THE ROYALS PREVAILED, 5-4.

"We just concentrated today to the last out. No matter what inning we are in, if we're down four runs or if we're up four runs, we need to play hard and finish the game."

Salvador Perez

GAME 3, OCTOBER 11
HOUSTON 4, KANSAS CITY 2

Dallas Keuchel had been unbeatable at home during the 2015 season, assembling a 15-0 record at Minute Maid Park. The Astros' bearded ace — who also notched the W in the AL Wild Card Game to get his team to this point — wasn't about to post his first loss once the Division Series moved to Houston for Game 3. But after a Lorenzo Cain homer gave the Royals a 1-0 lead, Keuchel and the Astros found themselves trailing.

The tide would soon turn, though, when an unlikely hero stepped to the plate. Catcher Jason Castro, known mostly for his work behind the plate, drove a one-out, two-strike single up the middle for his first career postseason hit, plating two runs and giving the Astros a 2-1 lead in the bottom of the fifth.

Houston would never look back. Carlos Gomez collected an RBI single in the sixth, and Chris Carter belted a solo homer in the seventh as part of a three-hit night. Alex Gordon led off the ninth with a solo home run to pull the Royals within two, but closer Luke Gregerson struck out Cain to end the game and bring Houston one win away from the ALCS.

	1	2	3	4	5	6	7	8	9	R	H	E
KANSAS CITY	0	0	0	1	0	0	0	0	1	2	7	0
HOUSTON	0	0	0	0	2	1	1	0	X	4	8	1

WP: Keuchel **LP:** Volquez **SV:** Gregerson
HR: HOU: Carter KC: Cain, Gordon

KEUCHEL'S LONE BLEMISH OF THE NIGHT CAME ON CAIN'S LONGBALL, AS HE STRUCK OUT SEVEN IN AS MANY INNINGS TO EARN THE WIN.

> **"The thing about these guys is they don't give up. They don't quit. It doesn't matter if you're down three in the ninth inning. It's a good group to be around in that respect, because you want guys fighting through to the last out."**
>
> *Royals Manager Ned Yost*

CAIN'S FOURTH-INNING HOME RUN GAVE THE ROYALS THE EARLY EDGE IN GAME 3, BUT THE ASTROS COUNTERED WITH FOUR RUNS IN FRONT OF A HOMETOWN CROWD.

GAME 4, OCTOBER 12
KANSAS CITY 9, HOUSTON 6

Facing elimination in Game 4, the Royals struck first on a second-inning, two-run Salvador Perez homer. But Houston was quick to answer with some longballs of its own.

Veteran Carlos Gomez and highly touted 21-year-old shortstop Carlos Correa went deep in the bottom of the second and third, respectively, to tie the game. With the Astros leading by one in the seventh, Correa would hit his second homer of the game before Colby Rasmus added another roundtripper to stake Houston to a 6-2 lead.

Just six outs from elimination, Kansas City would stage a furious comeback to lead off the eighth. Five consecutive singles cut their deficit to 6-4. With the bases loaded, Kendrys Morales hit a grounder up the middle that Correa misplayed for an error, allowing another two runs to score and tying the game. Four batters later, Alex Gordon's RBI groundout gave the Royals a 7-6 advantage.

In the ninth, Eric Hosmer knocked a two-run homer for good measure, while Wade Davis earned a two-inning save to send the series to a deciding Game 5 back at Kauffman Stadium.

	1	2	3	4	5	6	7	8	9	R	H	E
KANSAS CITY	0	2	0	0	0	0	0	5	2	9	8	0
HOUSTON	0	1	1	0	1	0	3	0	0	6	9	1

WP: Madson **LP:** Sipp **SV:** Davis **HR:** KC: Perez, Hosmer HOU: Gomez, Correa (2), Rasmus

GORDON COLLECTED AN RBI GROUNDOUT IN THE EIGHTH INNING TO GIVE THE ROYALS A 7-6 LEAD AT HOUSTON'S MINUTE MAID PARK.

"The mindset from the entire team was just make [every] at-bat count. We were down late [but] the mentality for this team is to never quit. The character we showed today, that's what a championship ballclub does."

Eric Hosmer

GAME 5, OCTOBER 14
KANSAS CITY 7, HOUSTON 2

Returning to their home turf for Game 5, the Royals sent prized midseason acquisition Johnny Cueto to the mound. The Astros countered with 19-game winner Collin McHugh.

Houston would jump out to an early lead on Luis Valbuena's two-run homer, but Kansas City got on the board two innings later on Eric Hosmer's RBI single. The home boys still trailed by one in the bottom of the fifth, though, when the first two Royals batters reached safely. After Houston called upon starter Mike Fiers in relief, Alex Rios greeted the right-hander with a two-run double down the left-field line that gave Kansas City a 3-2 lead.

On the other side, Cueto was superb, pitching eight innings of two-run ball and becoming the first pitcher since 2011 to retire the final 19 batters he faced in a postseason game. The Royals put the contest away in the eighth, when Kendrys Morales belted his third homer of the series, a three-run shot, to give the Royals a 7-2 lead. Wade Davis tossed a scoreless ninth to send Kansas City to back-to-back ALCS for the first time since 1984–85.

	1	2	3	4	5	6	7	8	9	R	H	E
HOUSTON	0	2	0	0	0	0	0	0	0	2	2	0
KANSAS CITY	0	0	0	1	3	0	0	3	X	7	8	0

WP: Cueto **LP:** McHugh
HR: KC: Morales HOU: Valbuena

IN FIVE ALDS GAMES, MORALES POSTED A 1.037 OPS WITH THREE HOME RUNS TO PUNCTUATE A DRAMATIC ROYALS COMEBACK.

"There's no doubt that Game 4 was an inspiration for me. When we gave up those runs and we came back and I saw everybody screaming in the dugout like we're not done yet, all I kept thinking was, 'If we can come back and win this game, I'll take care of business in Game 5.'"

Johnny Cueto

FIVE-YEAR ROYALS VETERAN MIKE MOUSTAKAS CELEBRATED KANSAS CITY'S SECOND CONSECUTIVE ALCS BERTH.

JARROD DYSON (ABOVE) AND HIS TEAMMATES (TOP) REVELED IN THE ROYALS' SECOND DIVISION SERIES VICTORY IN AS MANY YEARS. THE SPEEDSTER LEGGED OUT TWO STOLEN BASES IN THE ALDS AGAINST HOUSTON TO HELP HIS CLUB ADVANCE.

AMERICAN LEAGUE CHAMPIONSHIP SERIES

GAME 1, OCTOBER 16
KANSAS CITY 5, TORONTO 0

Since Kansas City's run to the World Series last year, Royals fans have become quite skilled at turning Kauffman Stadium's atmosphere into one of the greatest home-field advantages in baseball. And the raucous crowd helped do just that in the opening game of the ALCS. In the end, though, it was a pitcher not on last year's pennant-winning team who stole the show.

The Royals opened the scoring in the third with RBI hits from Alcides Escobar and Lorenzo Cain, then tacked on another run courtesy of a Salvador Perez solo home run. That proved to be all the run support Kansas City starter Edinson Volquez would need. The right-hander, who signed with the Royals in the offseason, was magnificent, earning his first postseason win after tossing six shutout innings and allowing just two hits. In the seventh, Volquez gave way to the bullpen, which threw three scoreless frames to complete the shutout, marking just the sixth time all season that the Blue Jays finished a game without pushing across a run.

	1	2	3	4	5	6	7	8	9	R	H	E
TORONTO	0	0	0	0	0	0	0	0	0	0	3	1
KANSAS CITY	0	0	2	1	0	0	0	2	X	5	8	1

WP: Volquez **LP:** Estrada
HR: KC: Perez

ROYALS FANS WERE OUT IN FULL FORCE FOR GAME 1. AFTER MISSING OUT ON OCTOBER BASEBALL FOR NEARLY 20 YEARS, KANSAS CITY PLAYED HOST TO TWO CONSECUTIVE ALCS.

"The fans give me a lot of energy.
I think hearing all those fans in the
stands calling my name 'Eddie, Eddie,
Eddie,' I [thought], 'Come on,
I have to do it for them.' And I did."

Edinson Volquez

GAME 2, OCTOBER 17
KANSAS CITY 6, TORONTO 3

Looking to avoid a 2-games-to-none deficit for the second consecutive postseason round, the Blue Jays sent former Cy Young winner David Price to the mound, and the move worked to perfection through the first six innings.

After allowing a leadoff single to Alcides Escobar on the first pitch of the game, the southpaw retired the next 18 batters he faced. Meanwhile, Toronto's offense plated three runs against Yordano Ventura on RBI doubles from Ryan Goins and Troy Tulowitzki, and a run-scoring base knock by Edwin Encarnacion.

But in the seventh inning, the Blue Jays' hopes of leaving Kansas City with a 1-1 series split were undone by a seemingly innocuous pop fly. Ben Zobrist led off the frame with a fly ball to shallow right field, but it fell between Goins and Jose Bautista, giving the Royals their first base runner since the opening inning. Things quickly unraveled for Price. He surrendered hits to four of the next six batters, the last of which was an Alex Gordon go-ahead RBI double. In total, Kansas City would score five runs in the inning before tallying another in the eighth for a 6-3 lead. In relief of Ventura, the Kansas City bullpen combined to pitch 3.2 scoreless innings, sending the Royals to Toronto with a 2-0 Series lead.

	1	2	3	4	5	6	7	8	9	R	H	E
TORONTO	0	0	1	0	0	2	0	0	0	3	10	0
KANSAS CITY	0	0	0	0	0	0	5	1	X	6	8	0

WP: Duffy **LP:** Price **SV:** Davis

ALEX RIOS CAPPED OFF THE ROYALS' FIVE-RUN SEVENTH INNING WITH AN RBI SINGLE TO CENTER FIELD, GIVING KANSAS CITY A TWO-RUN LEAD.

AFTER ALLOWING A SINGLE IN THE FIRST INNING, PRICE RETIRED 18 CONSECUTIVE BATTERS. BUT THE FORMER CY YOUNG WINNER WAS CHASED IN THE SEVENTH, AS THE ROYALS TAGGED HIM WITH FIVE RUNS ON FIVE HITS, BRINGING THE KAUFFMAN STADIUM CROWD TO ITS FEET.

"I felt like we needed to catch a break, and Zobrist's ball got things going. And once this lineup gets moving, it's one guy after another, and it was a big seventh inning."

Alex Gordon

TULOWITZKI (ABOVE) GAVE TORONTO A THREE-RUN LEAD WITH AN RBI DOUBLE IN THE SIXTH. BUT ZOBRIST (TOP) SINGLED TO LEAD OFF THE FOLLOWING FRAME, BEFORE COMING AROUND TO SCORE KANSAS CITY'S FIRST RUN OF THE GAME IN THE ROYALS' GO-AHEAD SEVENTH INNING.

GAME 3, OCTOBER 19
TORONTO 11, KANSAS CITY 8

With the series shifting to Toronto, Blue Jays fans hoped to provide the spark needed to lift their club back from a 2-games-to-none hole. It would not take long for the team to respond with plenty of fireworks for the hometown crowd, which had not experienced an ALCS game since 1993.

Clinging to a one-run lead in the third, the Blue Jays' potent offense came to life. Kevin Pillar's RBI double was sandwiched by homers from Troy Tulowitzki and Josh Donaldson, staking Toronto to a commanding 9-2 lead.

The Royals would battle back to scratch across eight runs, as Kendrys Morales hit his fourth postseason home run and Lorenzo Cain extended his playoff hitting streak to 12 games, tying a franchise record. Toronto's 11 runs, though, proved more than enough run support for starter Marcus Stroman,

who tossed 6.1 innings to earn his first postseason win, and the Blue Jays' bullpen.

But the star of the night was Ryan Goins. After committing a costly defensive gaffe in Game 2, he responded at the plate in a big way. Batting in the No. 9 spot, Goins hit a two-run single in the second before belting his first postseason homer three frames later to help Toronto secure its first win of the series.

	1	2	3	4	5	6	7	8	9	R	H	E
KANSAS CITY	1	0	1	0	2	0	0	0	4	**8**	**15**	**0**
TORONTO	0	3	6	0	1	0	0	1	X	**11**	**11**	**0**

WP: Stroman **LP:** Cueto
HR: TOR: Tulowitzki, Donaldson, Goins KC: Morales

AFTER DOMINATING IN THE CLINCHING GAME 5 OF THE ALDS, JOHNNY CUETO TOOK THE MOUND FOR THE ROYALS IN GAME 3. BUT THE RIGHT-HANDER STRUGGLED IN HIS FIRST ALCS START, ALLOWING EIGHT RUNS ON SIX HITS.

TULOWITZKI (TOP) WENT DEEP IN THE THIRD INNING FOR THE FIRST OF TORONTO'S THREE HOME RUNS IN THE GAME. THE BLUE JAYS WOULD TAKE A SEVEN-RUN LEAD INTO THE NINTH, WHEN MORALES (ABOVE, CENTER) HOMERED TO CUT THE DEFICIT TO THREE.

GAME 4, OCTOBER 20
KANSAS CITY 14, TORONTO 2

After Toronto lit up the scoreboard in the previous matchup, Game 4 was Kansas City's turn to flex its offensive muscle. Just two batters into the game, Ben Zobrist blasted a two-run homer and the Royals never looked back, scoring five in the opening two frames to chase Blue Jays starter R.A. Dickey.

Toronto would inch back into the contest with two runs in the third inning off Chris Young, who had split time between the rotation and bullpen during the 2015 campaign but got the ball to start Game 4.

With the game still hanging in the balance, the Royals scored four runs in the seventh before tacking on five more in the final two frames en route to a 15-hit, 14-run performance. Things got so bad for the Blue Jays that they called on Cliff Pennington to pitch in the ninth inning. He became the first full-time position player to pitch in a postseason game.

Young tossed 4.2 serviceable innings before Kansas City's relievers took over and combined to shut out the Blue Jays the rest of the way, sealing a 14-2 romp and positioning the Royals within one win of their second consecutive World Series berth.

	1	2	3	4	5	6	7	8	9	R	H	E
KANSAS CITY	4	1	0	0	0	0	4	3	2	14	15	0
TORONTO	0	0	2	0	0	0	0	0	0	2	7	0

WP: Hochevar **LP:** Dickey
HR: KC: Zobrist, Rios

YOUNG, WHO SPENT MOST OF THE SECOND HALF OF THE SEASON AS A RELIEVER, GOT THE BALL TO START GAME 4 AND TOSSED 4.2 INNINGS BEFORE EXITING WITH A 5-3 LEAD.

> "We were really focused on being productive collectively, and we're doing a pretty good job of that. Defensively we've been good. Offensively we've been even better."
>
> *Alex Rios*

PENNINGTON TOOK THE MOUND IN THE NINTH INNING, BECOMING THE FIRST POSITION PLAYER IN MLB HISTORY TO PITCH IN A POSTSEASON GAME.

"When you look at our lineup, there are no dead spots. The offensive sequence continues to flow from one to nine. These guys all have the ability to keep a rally going, which is big."

Royals Manager Ned Yost

LUKE HOCHEVAR (ABOVE) RECORDED THE LAST OUT OF THE FIFTH INNING TO EARN HIS FIRST CAREER POSTSEASON WIN. ZOBRIST AND ALCIDES ESCOBAR COMBINED FOR FOUR HITS, THREE RUNS SCORED AND SIX RBI AT THE TOP OF THE ROYALS' LINEUP.

GAME 5, OCTOBER 21
TORONTO 7, KANSAS CITY 1

Facing a 3-games-to-1 series deficit, the Blue Jays were not prepared to roll over quite yet. After Chris Colabello's solo shot in the second inning gave Toronto an early lead in front of its home crowd, both starting pitchers — the Blue Jays' Marco Estrada and the Royals' Edinson Volquez — exchanged zeroes for the next three frames.

Then, in the bottom of the sixth, the Blue Jays loaded the bases on two walks and a hit-by-pitch. Another base on balls to Edwin Encarnacion forced in a run to double Toronto's lead. Two batters later, Troy Tulowitzki lined a double off the center-field wall that cleared the bases to stretch the advantage to 5-0.

That proved to be more than enough support for Estrada, who tossed 7.2 frames of one-run ball. His only blemish came on a Salvador Perez solo shot in the eighth. Roberto Osuna then pitched a perfect ninth inning to secure the Blue Jays' victory.

	1	2	3	4	5	6	7	8	9	R	H	E
KANSAS CITY	0	0	0	0	0	0	0	1	0	1	4	0
TORONTO	0	1	0	0	0	4	1	1	X	7	8	0

WP: Estrada **LP:** Volquez
HR: TOR: Colabello KC: Perez

COLABELLO (FAR RIGHT) GAVE ESTRADA AN EARLY LEAD WITH A SOLO HOMER, AND THE RIGHT-HANDER CRUISED, ALLOWING JUST THREE HITS AND STRIKING OUT SEVEN OVER 7.2 INNINGS OF WORK.

VOLQUEZ DELIVERED A VALIANT EFFORT BUT COULD NOT MATCH HIS GAME 1 PERFORMANCE. HE SURRENDERED FIVE RUNS IN FIVE INNINGS AND WAS CHASED FROM THE GAME AFTER WALKING A BATTER WITH THE BASES LOADED IN THE SIXTH.

CHAMPIONSHIP SERIES

GAME 6, OCTOBER 23
KANSAS CITY 4, TORONTO 3

Returning to Kauffman Stadium for Game 6, Kansas City would try to secure a return trip to the World Series in a game that proved fraught with dramatics until the final out.

Solo home runs by the Royals' Ben Zobrist and Mike Moustakas and the Blue Jays' Jose Bautista put the score at 2-1 entering the bottom of the seventh, when Alex Rios delivered a clutch, two-out RBI single to add an insurance run for Kansas City. Then, in the top of the eighth, Bautista belted his second homer of the game, a two-run shot down the left-field line, to tie the score.

Lorenzo Cain walked to lead off the bottom half of the frame before Eric Hosmer ripped a single into the right-field corner. Running hard all the way around the bases, Cain beat the relay home after Bautista's throw went to second base, giving the Royals a 4-3 lead.

Wade Davis was tasked with getting the final three outs of the game. But the All-Star reliever, who had already recorded the final two outs of the eighth, allowed a leadoff single to Russell Martin. Pinch-runner Dalton Pompey promptly stole second and third to put the tying run 90 feet away with no outs. But after a walk to Kevin Pillar, Davis buckled down, striking out the next two batters before getting Josh Donaldson to ground out to end the game and clinch the Royals' second straight AL pennant.

	1	2	3	4	5	6	7	8	9	R	H	E
TORONTO	0	0	0	1	0	0	0	2	0	3	7	0
KANSAS CITY	1	1	0	0	0	0	1	1	X	4	9	0

WP: Davis **LP**: Osuna
HR: KC: Zobrist, Moustakas TOR: Bautista (2)

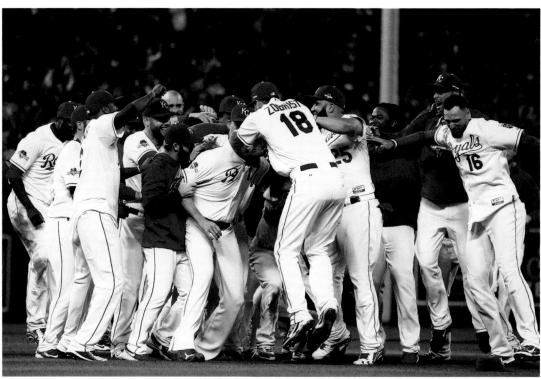

ZOBRIST AND HIS TEAMMATES STORMED THE INFIELD AFTER THE FINAL OUT. WITH THE WIN, THE ROYALS BECAME THE FIRST TEAM TO MAKE BACK-TO-BACK WORLD SERIES APPEARANCES SINCE THE 2010–11 TEXAS RANGERS.

"I think the fan base really got their share of the entertainment tonight. We were breathing easy once we finally saw that we had won the game. Just an incredible feeling to go from that low to winning it."

Ben Zobrist

DAVIS ALLOWED THE FIRST TWO BATTERS TO REACH BASE IN THE NINTH BUT QUICKLY NOTCHED TWO STRIKEOUTS BEFORE INDUCING A GROUND BALL OFF THE BAT OF DONALDSON TO END THE GAME, STRANDING THE TYING RUN ON THIRD.

MOUSTAKAS (ABOVE) WENT DEEP IN THE SECOND INNING FOR HIS FIRST POSTSEASON HOME RUN OF 2015, GIVING KANSAS CITY A 2–0 LEAD. THE SLUGGER DROVE IN FIVE RUNS DURING THE ALCS TO HELP THE ROYALS CLINCH THE PENNANT IN FRONT OF THEIR HOME FANS FOR THE SECOND CONSECUTIVE YEAR.

YORDANO VENTURA PITCHED INTO THE SIXTH AND ALLOWED JUST ONE RUN, WHILE ALCIDES ESCOBAR (FAR RIGHT) ADDED HIS TEAM-BEST 11TH HIT OF THE SERIES EN ROUTE TO TAKING HOME ALCS MVP HONORS.

"Last year at this time, we were so excited to be here. This year, from the first day of Spring Training, we *expected* to be here."

Royals Manager Ned Yost

CAIN RACED ALL THE WAY HOME FROM FIRST BASE ON HOSMER'S SINGLE TO SCORE THE GAME-WINNING RUN. IT WAS ONE OF EIGHT RUNS THE ROYALS' CENTER FIELDER AND 2014 ALCS MVP SCORED IN THE AL CHAMPIONSHIP SERIES.

WORLD SERIES

GAME 1, OCTOBER 27
ROYALS 5, METS 4

The Royals returned with a vengeance as Kauffman Stadium hosted Game 1 of the World Series for the second consecutive year. And they didn't waste a moment making their intentions known, as ALCS MVP Alcides Escobar knocked a fly ball to left-center field to lead off the game. It was a catchable ball, but when it dropped between left fielder Michael Conforto and center fielder Yoenis Cespedes, Escobar used his wheels to leg out an inside-the-park homer, sending the crowd into a frenzy.

"Any time you can get a run on the first pitch of the game, it definitely gets some momentum in your favor," said first baseman Eric Hosmer. "That's what we've been doing all year."

Royals starter Edinson Volquez kept New York off the board through the first three frames, but allowed one run apiece in each of the next three. In the top of the fifth, Mets leadoff man Curtis Granderson launched a 372-foot blast to put the visitors ahead.

It wasn't until Volquez came out of the game an inning later, though, that the 32-year-old starter learned that his father, Daniel, had passed away just hours earlier in his native Dominican Republic.

"We're going to pick [Volquez] up however we can," reliever Danny Duffy said after the game.

Kansas City did so even before the news broke, though, by plating two in the home half of the sixth, tying the game and setting the stage for some late-inning dramatics. But no one knew at that point just how late they would continue, ending well into the morning of Oct. 28. In fact, after 13 frames, the contest matched the record set by the 1916 and 2005 Fall Classics for the longest World Series Game 1 ever in terms of innings played.

After the Mets plated their fourth run on an eighth-inning error by Hosmer, the Royals entered the bottom of the ninth down by one. But with one out, homegrown stud Alex Gordon blasted a Jeurys Familia pitch into the depths of center field to even the score. With the homer, Gordon became the first player since Scott Brosius in 2001, and just the fifth in history, to tie a World Series game on a ninth-inning shot.

New York turned to a pair of starters to go the distance with the game in extra innings. Jon Niese allowed just one hit and struck out three in two innings of work before giving way to Bartolo Colon, who loaded the bases in the bottom of the 12th but escaped the jam unscathed. His fate would not be the same two frames later, though, as the Royals again filled the bases before walking off victorious. Hosmer's sacrifice fly to right field fittingly plated Escobar with the game-winning run.

"With no outs, I said, 'I'm going to win this game in this inning,'" Escobar said. "I was ready to score the run right there."

VOLQUEZ, WHOSE FATHER PASSED AWAY HOURS BEFORE THE START OF GAME 1, DELIVERED A VALIANT EFFORT ON THE MOUND, HOLDING THE METS TO THREE RUNS OVER SIX INNINGS.

	1	2	3	4	5	6	7	8	9	10	11	12	13	14	R	H	E
NEW YORK	0	0	0	1	1	1	0	1	0	0	0	0	0	0	4	11	1
KANSAS CITY	1	0	0	0	0	2	0	0	1	0	0	0	0	1	5	11	1

WP: Young **LP:** Colon
HR: KC: Escobar, Gordon NYM: Granderson

ALCS MVP ESCOBAR WASTED NO TIME CONTINUING HIS TORRID POSTSEASON HITTING. THE SHORTSTOP BELTED MATT HARVEY'S FIRST PITCH OF THE GAME TO DEEP LEFT-CENTER FIELD, AND AFTER IT BOUNCED AWAY FROM TWO METS OUTFIELDERS, HE SPRINTED AROUND THE BASES FOR AN INSIDE-THE-PARK HOME RUN.

"Every time I lose focus, I hear my dad saying, 'Concentrate. Focus on what you need to do to help this club win.' He's with me constantly. It's still fresh for me, and tonight brought back a tough time that I went through a month ago. Words can't describe my pain for Eddie."

Chris Young

NEVER SAY DIE

It was only fitting that the Royals and Mets would play 14 innings to kick off the 2015 Fall Classic, tying the record for the longest game in World Series history. After all, the unofficial mantra of both teams had been "Never Say Die" during the regular season, and it continued throughout their respective postseason runs.

"We definitely find our way into some crazy games, and we know how to make it exciting," said first baseman Eric Hosmer.

Hosmer's error on a Wilmer Flores ground ball in the eighth inning allowed the Mets to break a 3–3 tie, but all that did was set up Alex Gordon with a chance to gain redemption for his teammate via a game-tying home run in the bottom of the ninth. For Gordon, it wasn't about getting Hosmer off the hook, though.

"We don't do things like that," Gordon said. "We pick each other up, and we don't hang our heads when stuff like that happens. We understand that baseball is about adversity and overcoming it, and that's what he did."

Seizing the perfect opportunity to fully erase his rare miscue, Hosmer lofted a sac fly to end the game in the bottom of the 14th, sending the Royals to a Game 1 victory over a relentless opponent that took the lead on two different occasions.

"We always feel like we can come back and either make it a game or win," Gordon said. "I think it speaks to our team chemistry that we all pull together and we're all fighting for one thing, and that's to get the W."

AFTER THE ROYALS TIED THE GAME WITH TWO RUNS OFF HARVEY (TOP LEFT) IN THE SIXTH, NEW YORK REGAINED THE LEAD TWO FRAMES LATER. BUT GORDON'S NINTH-INNING HOMER (TOP RIGHT) SENT THE GAME INTO EXTRAS. IN THE 14TH, HOSMER (OPPOSITE) WOULD PLATE THE WALK-OFF RUN, ALLOWING KANSAS CITY TO CELEBRATE A SERIES-OPENING WIN.

"It was huge for us to win that. We threw a lot of pitchers out there, and I know it's going to hurt them way more than it hurt us, because we got the win."

Lorenzo Cain

GAME 2, OCTOBER 28
ROYALS 7, METS 1

A night after one of the wildest and longest World Series games in history, Johnny Cueto calmed things down drastically. The Royals' top trade deadline pick-up, who struggled toward the end of the regular season, posted one of the best pitching performances of the 2015 postseason. Cueto threw a complete-game two-hitter and retired 16 of the last 17 batters he faced in the Royals' 7-1 win.

"For him to come out, after how crazy and emotional last night was, and do that was awesome," Royals pitcher Chris Young said. "For him to take the game by the horns was incredible."

The Mets' young flame-throwing starting pitchers garnered much of the pre–World Series hype, but the Royals' ability to hit absolutely anything once again proved to be the more valuable asset.

"I just didn't make a pitch there in the fifth inning," said Mets starter Jacob deGrom. "They don't swing and miss, and they put the ball in play."

Kansas City hitters, in fact, swung and missed just six times in all of Game 2 — they didn't swing and miss even once against 32 deGrom fastballs — to stake themselves to a 2-games-to-none Series lead. deGrom appeared in command through three hitless frames, but the Royals batted around in a four-run fifth inning.

Alcides Escobar continued his red-hot hitting, driving in the first Kansas City run in the fifth with a single to center, then tripling in a run in the eighth. Manager Ned Yost refers to Escobar's ability to put the ball in play as "Esky Magic," and Escobar lived up to the reputation by extending his streak to 12 straight postseason games with a base hit. "We saw two great pitchers who throw 95," Escobar said. "Nobody likes facing that."

The Royals may claim to dislike facing the Mets' heat, but they certainly proved through the first two games that they can handle it. First baseman Eric Hosmer collected two hits and plated two runs in the contest, pushing his postseason RBI total to 15. And with a walk in the seventh inning, Lorenzo Cain extended his streak to 17 postseason games reaching base safely.

"We saw (deGrom) great tonight," Cain said. "We got good pitches and had great at-bats."

Although two-thirds of their super-hero starting pitcher trio failed to win either of the first two Fall Classic games, the Mets could find some comfort in the fact that the Series was headed to New York, where they hoped to bring the prize back within reach.

"It will be nice to get to our house," said David Wright. "I'm sure the fans are going to be going crazy."

	1	2	3	4	5	6	7	8	9	R	H	E
NEW YORK	0	0	0	1	0	0	0	0	0	1	2	1
KANSAS CITY	0	0	0	0	4	0	0	3	X	7	10	0

WP: Cueto LP: deGrom

"Put the ball in play, and they say good things happen. It's a tribute to the hitters we have."
Chris Young

CUETO WAS DOMINANT FROM
START TO FINISH IN GAME 2,
ALLOWING JUST FIVE METS TO
REACH BASE ALL NIGHT. HE
BECAME THE FIRST AL PITCHER
TO THROW A COMPLETE GAME IN
THE WORLD SERIES SINCE 1991.

INSURMOUNTABLE

The October of dominant craftsmanship on the mound continued in Game 2. Billed as a matchup of All-Stars, reigning NL Rookie of the Year Jacob deGrom faced off against the Royals' prized midseason acquisition, Johnny Cueto. And just as teammate Eric Hosmer had predicted a night earlier, the home club's ace was lights out.

"Obviously both teams used a lot of the bullpen," Hosmer said following the marathon affair that was Game 1. "So we're counting on Cueto to go out there tomorrow and give us a great outing."

His complete-game performance provided exactly what the Royals ordered, as the Mets scratched out a mere two hits against the 29-year-old, who secured his second victory of the 2015 postseason. He also joined elite company, tossing the first World Series two-hitter since Greg Maddux in 1995.

"I trust in Cueto," said Alcides Escobar. "I know every time he goes to the mound, he can throw like he did tonight."

Although not as dominant, deGrom traded zeroes with Cueto through the first three frames and didn't allow Kansas City to get on the board until its offense rallied for four runs in the bottom of the fifth. The shaky outing was certainly uncharacteristic of the Mets' staff, as no starter had permitted four or more runs in a game since Sept. 22.

"Jake came out throwing the ball great, and they grinded him out," said David Wright. "They just found some holes."

"In that situation," echoed backstop Travis d'Arnaud, "you just tip your cap and try to get the next one."

"We're a fastball-hitting team, and it showed again tonight."

Lorenzo Cain

KANSAS CITY EXCELLED IN ALL ASPECTS DURING GAME 2. ESCOBAR (OPPOSITE), HOSMER (BELOW) AND MIKE MOUSTAKAS (ABOVE, LEFT) ALL DROVE IN RUNS, WITH THE FORMER TWO ALSO COMING AROUND TO SCORE IN THE CLUB'S FOUR-RUN FIFTH INNING. IT WAS MORE THAN ENOUGH OFFENSIVE SUPPORT FOR CUETO AND THE ROYALS' DEFENSE, INCLUDING SECOND BASEMAN BEN ZOBRIST, WHO HELPED TURN AN INNING-ENDING DOUBLE PLAY IN THE SECOND TO KEEP THE CONTEST SCORELESS.

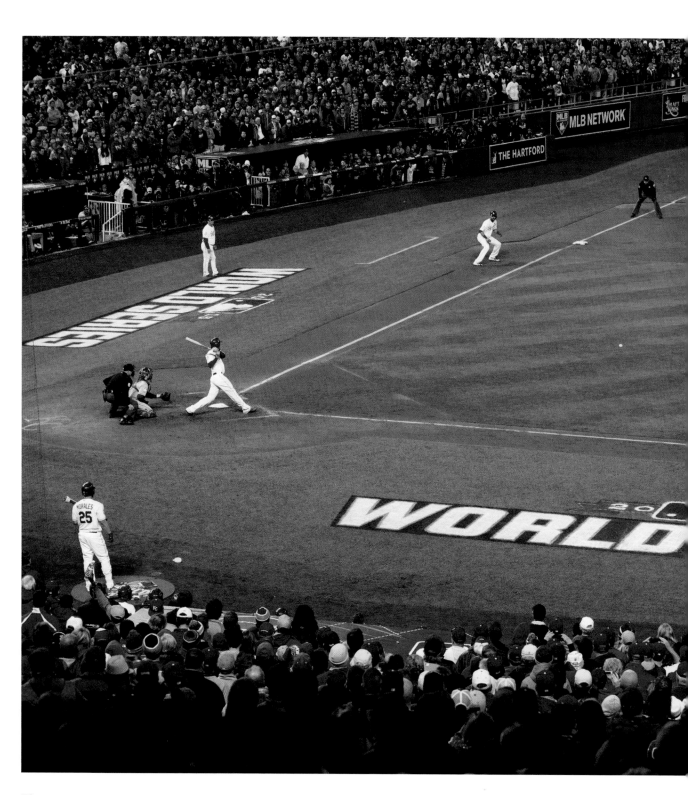

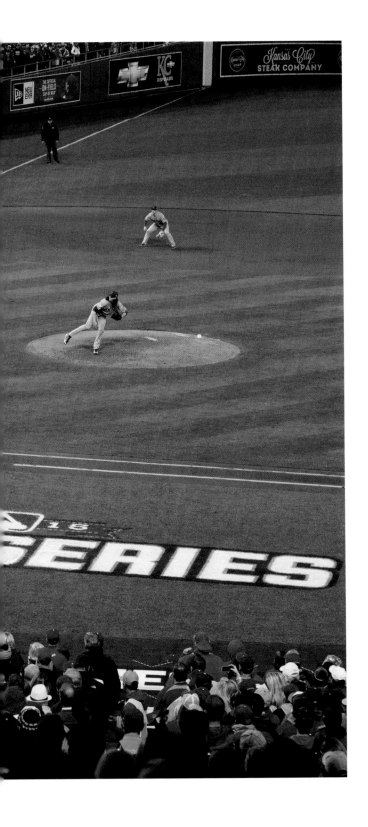

"Any time you have opportunities with guys on base, you've got to make the most out of it. As an offense, we had to do anything we could to figure out how to get to deGrom. I'm just glad it worked out for us."

Eric Hosmer

GAME 3, OCTOBER 30
METS 9, ROYALS 3

New York truly was in a Mets state of mind on Friday night. A packed house — featuring none other than National Anthem singer Billy Joel — energized the hometown club at Citi Field, which was hosting the first World Series game in the ballpark's six-year history. And although starting pitcher Noah Syndergaard surrendered three Kansas City runs in the first two frames, he soon brought the hammer down, at one point retiring 12 straight Royals batters before exiting the game after the sixth.

"He didn't have his best stuff, but that just shows the type of pitcher he is," said Addison Reed, who came on in relief in the top of the seventh. "He didn't have close to his dominant stuff, and it could have spiraled out of control, but he didn't let it."

Indeed, Thor allowed a hard-hit double to No. 2 hitter Ben Zobrist, who later came around to score the game's first run. But New York quickly came to his aid, as leadoff man Curtis Granderson singled, reaching base in his ninth game this postseason. Mets veteran David Wright then played hero, launching a home run well into the left-field stands.

"We got a big hit from our captain," said rookie Michael Conforto, who began the game in left field.

The Mets also got some stellar work on defense beginning in the top of the second, as Conforto came up firing on an Alex Rios double, nabbing runner Alex Gordon at third base. Gordon was originally ruled safe, but Wright signaled for the team to challenge, and the call was overturned as Wright's foot appeared to block Gordon's hand from immediately touching the bag.

"It's huge," said Reed. "It could have been a game changer, could have shifted the momentum to their side. But it kept it on our side, and we really fed off it."

From that point on, Syndergaard settled down on the mound. He helped his own cause in the bottom of the third, smacking a single. Granderson then made it count, pulling a two-run shot to the right-field corner that barely cleared the fence. The outfielder is now just the sixth player in Mets history with multiple home runs in a single World Series.

Two innings later, the Royals also made history when they brought in Raul Mondesi to pinch-hit for reliever Danny Duffy. With the at-bat, Mondesi became the first player ever to make his Major League debut in the Fall Classic. Unfortunately for the visitors, though, neither he nor the rest of the lineup could muster much against Syndergaard and a trio of Mets relievers, who got all the help they needed with a four-run sixth.

"You've got to give credit to the fans," said catcher Travis d'Arnaud, "for giving us that extra energy that we had tonight."

	1	2	3	4	5	6	7	8	9	R	H	E
KANSAS CITY	1	2	0	0	0	0	0	0	0	3	7	0
NEW YORK	2	0	2	1	0	4	0	0	X	9	12	0

WP: Syndergaard **LP:** Ventura
NYM: Wright, Granderson

GRAMMY AWARD–WINNING ARTIST BILLY JOEL SANG THE NATIONAL ANTHEM BEFORE GAME 3. NED YOST AND MIKE MOUSTAKAS (OPPOSITE) SHOOK HANDS WHILE ESCOBAR LOOKED ON DURING PLAYER INTRODUCTIONS.

"In that situation, I'm just looking for a strike. I'm not looking for a ball at my head. It's not 88; it's 98. That's no good. Everybody in this room doesn't like it."

Alcides Escobar

WARNING SHOT

Mets starter Noah Syndergaard set the tone early in Game 3 with a 98-mph heater. His fastball sent electricity through Citi Field when he threw it high and tight to knock down Royals shortstop Alcides Escobar on the very first pitch of the game. Since Syndergaard mentioned having "a few tricks" up his sleeve for Escobar during an interview the day before, the Royals couldn't help but assume it was no accident.

"Obviously no one's happy about that," said Kansas City first baseman Eric Hosmer. "Anytime one of your teammates gets his head thrown at, it's not going to go over well."

When asked if he thought there was intent, Hosmer replied, "No question."

Escobar had made a habit of swinging at the first pitch, and collected yet another base knock to extend his postseason hitting streak to 13 games, even after looking a little shaken from the pitch that buzzed his head.

For his part, Syndergaard wasn't exactly hiding his intentions after the game.

"I know how aggressive they are, and I didn't want them to feel too comfortable out there," the 23-year-old rookie said. "It's my plate out there; it's not theirs. If they have a problem with me throwing inside, then they can meet me 60 feet, 6 inches away."

Syndergaard's catcher, Travis d'Arnaud, talked after the game about the need to establish the inside part of the plate, while reliever Tyler Clippard reacted simply, "I liked it. That's just playing the game."

Royals players clearly viewed the situation differently. "It looked like there was intent," third baseman Mike Moustakas said. "He had pretty good command after that."

"[Syndergaard] did a good job to get ahead a lot with his off-speed, then used his fastball later in the counts."

Eric Hosmer

COUNTERCLOCKWISE FROM TOP LEFT: THE ROYALS STARTED STRONG WITH ZOBRIST'S DOUBLE IN THE FIRST INNING. IN THE TOP OF THE SECOND, RIOS HIT A SINGLE, BRINGING HOME SALVADOR PEREZ, AND LATER SCORED ON A PASSED BALL. FANS HELD STAND UP TO CANCER SIGNS IN HONOR OF CANCER VICTIMS AND SURVIVORS AT THE END OF THE FIFTH INNING. RELIEVER LUKE HOCHEVAR INDUCED A DANIEL MURPHY GROUNDOUT IN THE FIFTH.

LUCAS DUDA TRIED
SLIDING INTO FIRST BASE,
BUT COULDN'T BEAT THE
THROW.

GAME 4, OCTOBER 31
ROYALS 5, METS 3

The Mets were just five outs away from evening the Fall Classic at two games apiece, but the Royals' trademark persistence paid off yet again.

These two teams reached the Fall Classic thanks in large part to their solid defensive play, but both teams had their sloppy moments in Game 4. The Royals weren't charged with any errors, but right fielder Alex Rios seemed to think there were three outs when he caught a third-inning fly ball for the second out, on which Wilmer Flores tagged from third to score. The Mets made two errors, and the second gaffe proved costly, as Daniel Murphy allowed a ground ball to skip by him in the eighth inning, sending home Ben Zobrist to tie the score at 3-3. That opened the door for a three-run rally and eventual 5-3 margin of victory for Kansas City.

"I tried to one-hand it, and it probably deserved to be two-handed," Murphy said of his error. "I just misplayed it. It's frustrating because we put ourselves in a position to win a ballgame today."

As they have done to so many teams, the Royals took full advantage of the miscue.

"Momentum changed in our favor there," first baseman Eric Hosmer said. "It was a huge break, and we were able to capitalize on it. Perez put together a great at-bat with two strikes. Everyone is doing their part, putting together great at-bats. We never think we're out of a game."

The Mets got on the board first when rookie Michael Conforto launched a towering home run to right field to lead off the third inning. Flores then singled, and eventually came around to score on the aforementioned Curtis Granderson sac fly to Rios. After Alex Gordon's RBI single in the top of the fifth inning cut the lead to 2-1, Conforto led off the bottom of the fifth with his second dinger of the game, becoming the youngest Met ever to homer in a World Series game and the fourth-youngest player ever to post a multi-homer post-season contest. But a Zobrist double and Lorenzo Cain RBI single in the sixth made the score 3-2, and that proved to be insufficient as the game was handed over to the Kansas City bullpen. After Danny Duffy relieved starter Chris Young and yielded Conforto's second home run in the fifth, the Royals'

bullpen closed out the game with four scoreless innings, including two by stopper Wade Davis, who earned the save.

Alcides Escobar led off the game with a single, his 22nd base knock this postseason, and extended his hitting streak to 14 postseason games. Salvador Perez went 3 for 4 with two RBI, and improved his ledger to hitting safely in nine of his first 11 career World Series games.

In the end, the Mets' Game 4 lead never felt safe, and the Royals stayed close enough to do what they do best.

"You can never count this team out," said reliever Duffy. "We do whatever we have to do to win."

	1	2	3	4	5	6	7	8	9	R	H	E
KANSAS CITY	0	0	0	0	1	1	0	3	0	5	9	0
NEW YORK	0	0	2	0	1	0	0	0	0	3	6	2

WP: Madson **LP:** Clippard **SV:** Davis
HR: NYM: Conforto (2)

GAME 4 WAS CHARACTERIZED BY METS' ERRORS. MURPHY (OPPOSITE) MISSED A GROUND BALL THAT OPENED THE DOOR FOR KANSAS CITY TO TIE THE GAME, AND EVENTUALLY TRIUMPH. MIKE MOUSTAKAS (LEFT) MADE A LEAPING CATCH TO TAKE AWAY A BASE-HIT.

"We're just trying to make things happen. Put together good at-bats. Put together big innings. Then, when they make a mistake, take advantage of it. That's what championship teams do."

Eric Hosmer

BATTLE OF THE BULLPENS

Game 4 starters Chris Young and Steven Matz posted nearly identical stat lines on Saturday night, striking out three and five batters in four and five innings of work, respectively. But once they exited, nearly half of the game fell on the bullpen's shoulders.

The Mets and Royals combined to cycle through 12 pitchers at Citi Field, 10 of which were relievers. Kansas City turned to its 'pen first, but the home club tagged Danny Duffy for a solo home run in the bottom of the fifth. From there, however, Luke Hochevar and Ryan Madson each threw hitless frames, while the Royals' offense began to claw its way back into the game.

"We knew we were in for a grind when they went to the bullpen early," said Mets captain David Wright. "You have to have more of a cushion when you get to that bullpen. One run [advantage] against this team, that's not safe."

And sure enough, in the eighth, Royals skipper Ned Yost called for closer Wade Davis to lock down a two-inning save. The right-hander allowed just a pair of hits and whiffed two to seal the Royals' third victory of the Series.

The Mets' relievers made the visitors work for it, though. In the sixth, Manager Terry Collins turned to regular-season starters Jon Niese and Bartolo Colon, and the pair combined for a scoreless inning. Addison Reed then added a one-K frame, but after Tyler Clippard walked two, closer Jeurys Familia trotted in from the 'pen in the eighth, seeking his sixth save of this postseason. On the first batter he faced, though, a Daniel Murphy error caused things to unravel quickly.

Hansel Robles got the ball for the ninth and struck out two, but Davis didn't allow the Mets to edge back in. As Duffy put it simply, "We've got to finish the job."

"We've got to finish the job, doing what we know how to do best. At the end of the day, it's baseball, the same game we played when we were little."

Danny Duffy

AFTER GAME 4, THE ROYALS WERE A WIN AWAY FROM THE TITLE. RIOS (RIGHT) MADE A GREAT A CATCH IN THE FIRST INNING. IN THE EIGHTH, THE ROYALS WERE QUICK TO POUNCE AFTER MURPHY'S ERROR: ONLY MOMENTS LATER, MOUSTAKAS (OPPOSITE) LACED AN RBI SINGLE, AND PEREZ (BELOW) KNOCKED IN AN INSURANCE RUN. ROYALS MANAGER NED YOST THEN CALLED IN DAVIS (BOTTOM) TO CLOSE THE DEAL.

PEREZ POKED AN RBI SINGLE
IN THE TOP OF THE EIGHTH
INNING, ALLOWING HOSMER
TO SCORE TO PUT KANSAS
CITY AHEAD FOR GOOD, 5–3.

GAME 5, NOVEMBER 1
ROYALS 7, METS 2

While Game 1 remained the marathon of the Series at 14 innings, the Mets hosted a 12-frame Game 5 just hours after the end of the actual New York City Marathon. New Yorkers reveled in the double feature, as Citi Field welcomed 44,859 fans, the largest crowd (2013 All-Star Game aside) in ballpark history.

But just when the Mets seemed to have all but locked up a victory to send the Series back to Kansas City, things came apart at the seams. In the top of the ninth, Matt Harvey returned to the mound in search of a complete game. But the Royals quickly erased the Mets' lead, which had held steady since Curtis Granderson homered to lead off the home half of the first, by scratching out a pair of runs in a way only they know how. After Harvey issued a leadoff walk to Lorenzo Cain, the speedy outfielder stole second and came around to score on an Eric Hosmer double, which chased the Mets' starter from the game and brought the score within one. Hosmer then took third on a Mike Moustakas groundout before making the decision that changed the course of the game.

When eventual World Series MVP Salvador Perez grounded out to David Wright, the Mets' third baseman looked back at Hosmer to hold him near the bag. But as soon as Wright released his throw to first, Hosmer broke for home. Lucas Duda's throw went wide, and Hosmer crossed the plate with the tying run.

"As soon as his head turned to go to first base, I just decided it's an opportunity for us to maybe steal a run," said Hosmer. "With a guy like [closer Jeurys] Familia on the mound, you know hits are hard to come by. That's our style of play — to be aggressive — so we just had to take a chance right there."

The play opened the door for the Royals' eighth come-from-behind victory of the postseason, and the seventh in which they came back from a multi-run deficit. After two scoreless frames of extras, Kansas City broke the game open with a five-run rally in the top of the 12th, which began on a Perez single. Jarrod Dyson entered the game as a pinch-runner and promptly stole second, before pinch-hitter Christian Colon knocked an RBI single in his first at-bat of the entire postseason.

"He's a clutch-type player," Manager Ned Yost said of Colon. "He's going to give you everything that he's got. And for him to come through tonight and get the big hit, it was special."

Meanwhile, a trio of Royals relievers — including Kelvin Herrera, who whiffed three in as many innings of work — combined to shut down the Mets' bats from the seventh on. They held New York to just a pair of hits through six scoreless frames, sending Kansas City home with the crown.

"It's just unbelievable," said Hosmer, "to realize you're a world champion."

EDINSON VOLQUEZ (ABOVE) HONORED HIS FATHER'S RECENT PASSING WITH A STELLAR PITCHING PERFORMANCE. FOR THE SECOND TIME IN THE WORLD SERIES, THE METS-ROYALS TOOK THE GAME INTO EXTRA INNINGS. WHEN THE ROYALS SECURED THE LEAD FOR THE FIRST TIME IN 12 INNINGS, THERE WAS NO GIVING IT UP. SALVADOR PEREZ (OPPOSITE) CELEBRATED BY DOUSING NED YOST.

	1	2	3	4	5	6	7	8	9	10	11	12	R	H	E
KANSAS CITY	0	0	0	0	0	0	0	0	2	0	0	5	7	10	1
NEW YORK	1	0	0	0	0	1	0	0	0	0	0	0	2	4	2

WP: Hochevar **LP:** Reed
HR: NYM: Granderson

"This is just too good of a group, too good of a team not to be remembered as world champions. We obviously accomplished a lot last year, but to come back and finish the job, to have this group be able to go down in history, it's unbelievable."

Eric Hosmer

MOST BRUISED, MOST VALUABLE

After countless piercing foul balls off his mask, fingers and every other body part that took a beating this season, Salvador Perez earned World Series MVP honors, which surely made every ache seem a lot less painful.

"I think it's part of my job," Perez said, "to take a foul ball or wild pitch. (And if I'm knocked out of a game) I feel like I'm not going to do anything to help my team win."

Royals Manager Ned Yost, a former catcher himself, said he had just one regret as his team clinched its first title since 1985: the fact that he had to pinch-run for Perez in the 12th inning after he had led off with a single. "I really wish Sal could have been out there to jump in Wade's arms when he got the final out," Yost said. "But it opened up the door for us to score five."

Perez was, however, on the field to do plenty to help Kansas City claim the crown. In addition to his great, and rugged, work behind the plate, he went 8 for 22 for a .364 average at the dish, with two doubles, two RBI and three runs scored. The backstop has now notched a hit in 10 of his 12 career World Series games, and although he doesn't quite have the wheels to steal a base like pinch-runner Jarrod Dyson did in the 12th, it was Perez's hit that started yet another Royals' late-inning rally.

"You guys know what we do all season," Perez, who signed with Kansas City at 16 years old, told reporters after the Game 5 celebration. "We never quit. We never put our heads down. We never think the game is over. We always compete to the last out. And that's what we did tonight."

"In 2015, Kansas City is No. 1. Who cares about what happened last year?"

Salvador Perez

IN GAME 5, THE METS HELD A 2–0 LEAD UNTIL THE NINTH INNING. AFTER STEALING SECOND BASE, LORENZO CAIN (TOP, LEFT) SCORED ON A DOUBLE FROM ERIC HOSMER, WHO RECEIVED A HERO'S WELCOME (ABOVE) AFTER SCORING THE GAME–TYING RUN ON PEREZ'S GROUNDOUT.

POSTSEASON STATS

NO.	PLAYER		W	L	ERA	SO	BB	SV
	PITCHERS							
47	JOHNNY CUETO		2	1	5.40	19	10	0
17	WADE DAVIS		1	0	0.00	18	3	4
41	DANNY DUFFY		1	0	6.00	9	0	0
40	KELVIN HERRERA		1	0	0.66	22	3	0
44	LUKE HOCHEVAR		2	0	0.00	4	1	0
46	RYAN MADSON		2	0	5.40	15	3	0
39	KRIS MEDLEN		0	0	3.00	8	1	0
45	FRANKLIN MORALES		0	0	19.29	2	1	0
30	YORDANO VENTURA		0	2	6.43	22	8	0
36	EDINSON VOLQUEZ		1	2	3.77	23	18	0
32	CHRIS YOUNG		1	0	2.87	18	6	0

NO.	PLAYER		AB	H	AVG	HR	RBI	OBP
	CATCHERS							
9	DREW BUTERA		1	0	.000	0	0	.500
13	SALVADOR PEREZ		58	15	.259	4	8	.328
	INFIELDERS							
24	CHRISTIAN COLON		1	1	1.000	0	1	1.000
2	ALCIDES ESCOBAR		70	23	.329	1	9	.347
35	ERIC HOSMER		66	14	.212	1	17	.236
21	RAUL MONDESI		1	0	.000	0	0	.000
25	KENDRYS MORALES		51	13	.255	4	10	.304
8	MIKE MOUSTAKAS		65	14	.215	1	8	.257
18	BEN ZOBRIST		66	20	.303	2	6	.365
	OUTFIELDERS							
6	LORENZO CAIN		62	16	.258	1	11	.365
1	JARROD DYSON		4	0	.000	0	0	.000
4	ALEX GORDON		54	13	.241	2	6	.349
0	TERRANCE GORE		0	0	–	0	0	–
16	PAULO ORLANDO		11	3	.273	0	1	.250
15	ALEX RIOS		48	13	.271	1	6	.314

BIRTH OF
THE ROYALS

After the Athletics left Kansas City for Oakland following the 1967 campaign, Major League Baseball granted the abandoned city one of its four expansion teams to begin play in 1969. Local businessman Ewing Kauffman won the bidding rights for the club and named it the Royals, a nod to the American Royal livestock show held annually in Kansas City since 1899.

The Royals recorded their first winning season in 1971 and moved into the new Royals Stadium two years later. The team went on to take the Western Division title for three straight years in the '70s, and won the American League pennant in 1980. That season, the Royals competed for their first World Series title before finally taking the crown in 1985 under Manager Dick Howser. The decade featured three playoff berths in all, while players like Bo Jackson and Bret Saberhagen blossomed into stars.

The franchise faced some tough times in the '90s, including the death of Kauffman and his wife, Muriel, as well as the loss of beloved reliever Dan Quisenberry. Future Hall of Famer George Brett retired in 1993, but before his departure, he broke the 3,000-hit barrier.

The Glass family took over as the team's owners in the new millennium, and Kansas City shined in 2003, posting its first winning season in nearly a decade. The team's success was due in large part to Carlos Beltran, the first player in Royals history to record a 20-homer, 40-steal season.

After several mediocre years, the 2009 season opened with a rededicated Kauffman Stadium and culminated with pitcher Zack Greinke receiving the AL Cy Young Award. Six years later, in 2015, the team reached the playoffs for the second consecutive season en route to winning the second World Series title in franchise history.

HOWSER LED THE ROYALS TO THEIR FIRST WORLD SERIES TITLE IN 1985. MORE THAN TWO DECADES LATER, ON OPENING DAY IN 2009, THE ROYALS UNVEILED A BRONZE STATUE OF THE FORMER MANAGER IN THE NEWLY RENOVATED KAUFFMAN STADIUM.

KANSAS CITY ROYALS POSTSEASON HISTORY

THE ROYALS FIRST HOSTED THE WORLD SERIES IN 1980, THEIR 12TH YEAR AS A MAJOR LEAGUE FRANCHISE. ALTHOUGH KANSAS CITY LOST TO PHILADELPHIA, THE SEASON STARTED A RUN OF SUCCESS THAT INCLUDED THREE MORE POSTSEASON TRIPS IN FIVE YEARS.

1976

ALCS
NEW YORK YANKEES 3, ROYALS 2
> **Oct. 9** Yankees 4 at Royals 1
> **Oct. 10** Yankees 3 at Royals 7
> **Oct. 12** Royals 3 at Yankees 5
> **Oct. 13** Royals 7 at Yankees 4
> **Oct. 14** Royals 6 at Yankees 7

1977

ALCS
NEW YORK YANKEES 3, ROYALS 2
> **Oct. 5** Royals 7 at Yankees 2
> **Oct. 6** Royals 2 at Yankees 6
> **Oct. 7** Yankees 2 at Royals 6
> **Oct. 8** Yankees 6 at Royals 4
> **Oct. 9** Yankees 5 at Royals 3

1978

ALCS

NEW YORK YANKEES 3, ROYALS 1
- **Oct. 3** Yankees 7 at Royals 1
- **Oct. 4** Yankees 4 at Royals 10
- **Oct. 6** Royals 5 at Yankees 6
- **Oct. 7** Royals 1 at Yankees 2

1980

ALCS

ROYALS 3, NEW YORK YANKEES 0
- **Oct. 8** Yankees 2 at Royals 7
- **Oct. 9** Yankees 2 at Royals 3
- **Oct. 10** Royals 4 at Yankees 2

WORLD SERIES

PHILADELPHIA PHILLIES 4, ROYALS 2
- **Oct. 14** Royals 6 at Phillies 7
- **Oct. 15** Royals 4 at Phillies 6
- **Oct. 17** Phillies 3 at Royals 4
- **Oct. 18** Phillies 3 at Royals 5
- **Oct. 19** Phillies 4 at Royals 3
- **Oct. 21** Royals 1 at Phillies 4

When the Royals dispatched the Yankees in the 1980 AL Championship Series after New York had beaten Kansas City in the same round each year from 1976–78, they became the first American League expansion team to reach the World Series. The heart and soul of Kansas City's squad was George Brett, who batted .390 during the regular season. The team also featured switch-hitter Willie Wilson, 20-game winner Dennis Leonard and star reliever Dan Quisenberry.

Kansas City faced a difficult Fall Classic matchup, as the Phillies employed stars like NL MVP Mike Schmidt and Cy Young Award winner Steve Carlton. In Game 1, Philadelphia capitalized on a five-run third inning and held on for a 7-6 win. Kansas City would take a two-run lead into the eighth inning of Game 2, but the Phillies plated four in the frame en route to a 6-4 win.

As the Series moved to Kansas City, momentum began to shift. After

OTIS LED THE ROYALS WITH A .478 AVERAGE IN THE 1980 WORLD SERIES. THE SLUGGING OUTFIELDER COLLECTED 11 HITS, INCLUDING TWO DOUBLES AND THREE HOME RUNS, AND SEVEN RBI IN THE SIX-GAME CLASSIC.

home runs from Brett, Schmidt and Amos Otis, Game 3 went into extra innings. In the 10th, Willie Aikens' RBI single gave the Royals a 4-3 win. Kansas City carried that momentum into Game 4, during which a four-run first inning catapulted the club to a 5-3 victory.

In Game 5, the Royals had staked themselves to a 3-2 lead, but Schmidt led off the ninth inning with a single and scored on a double to tie it. After a bunt and infield hit, the Phillies took a one-run lead. Kansas City threatened with the bases loaded in the bottom of the frame, but Tug McGraw struck out Jose Cardenal to end the game.

Back in Philadelphia, the Phillies had a chance to clinch the world title in front of their home fans. Schmidt, the eventual World Series MVP, drove in two runs in the third inning of Game 6, which would prove to be all the runs the club needed. McGraw came on to escape a jam in the eighth and closed out the contest in the ninth, securing the club's first title in franchise history.

1981

ALDS
OAKLAND ATHLETICS 3, ROYALS 0
  Oct. 6 A's 4 at Royals 0
  Oct. 7 A's 2 at Royals 1
  Oct. 9 Royals 1 at A's 4

1984

ALCS
DETROIT TIGERS 3, ROYALS 0
  Oct. 2 Tigers 8 at Royals 1
  Oct. 3 Tigers 5 at Royals 3
  Oct. 5 Royals 0 at Tigers 1

1985

ALCS
ROYALS 4, TORONTO BLUE JAYS 3
  Oct. 8 Royals 1 at Blue Jays 6
  Oct. 9 Royals 5 at Blue Jays 6
  Oct. 11 Blue Jays 5 at Royals 6
  Oct. 12 Blue Jays 3 at Royals 1
  Oct. 13 Blue Jays 0 at Royals 2
  Oct. 15 Royals 5 at Blue Jays 3
  Oct. 16 Royals 6 at Blue Jays 2

WORLD SERIES
ROYALS 4, ST. LOUIS CARDINALS 3
  Oct. 19 Cardinals 3 at Royals 1
  Oct. 20 Cardinals 4 at Royals 2
  Oct. 22 Royals 6 at Cardinals 1
  Oct. 23 Royals 0 at Cardinals 3
  Oct. 24 Royals 6 at Cardinals 1
  Oct. 26 Cardinals 1 at Royals 2
  Oct. 27 Cardinals 0 at Royals 11

A year after they were swept in the Championship Series, the Royals won a seven-game ALCS matchup against the Toronto Blue Jays to earn their second-ever Fall Classic appearance.

In the World Series, Cardinals pitchers John Tudor and Danny Cox combined to surrender just three runs in their Game 1 and 2 starts, respectively, as the Cardinals took the first two games in Kansas City. But when the Series moved to St. Louis, the Royals rallied. Frank White homered in Game 3, while Bret Saberhagen tossed a complete game in a 6-1, victory. The Cardinals moved within just one win of a world title after Tudor's complete-game shutout in Game 4, but the Royals then took the final contest in St. Louis, forcing a Game 6.

Back in Kansas City, that contest remained scoreless through seven. The Cards plated a run in the eighth, but the Royals mounted a comeback in the ninth. Jorge Orta led of with an infield

SABERHAGEN WAS NAMED SERIES MVP AFTER GOING THE DISTANCE IN BOTH OF HIS 1985 FALL CLASSIC STARTS. THE RIGHT-HANDER ALLOWED JUST ONE RUN IN HIS TWO VICTORIES, WHICH INCLUDED A SHUTOUT IN THE CLINCHING GAME 7.

single after a controversial call at first, before Kansas City loaded the bases for pinch-hitter Dane Iorg, who delivered a two-run, walk-off single. The Royals ensured that the deciding Game 7 would not be nearly as dramatic. Already staked to a 5-0 lead, Kansas City scored six more runs in the fifth. It was more than enough for Series MVP Saberhagen, who again went the distance as the Royals celebrated their first World Series title.

2014

WILD CARD
ROYALS vs. OAKLAND ATHLETICS
 Sept. 30 Athletics 8 at Royals 9

ALDS
ROYALS 3, LOS ANGELES ANGELS 0
 Oct. 2 Royals 3 at Angels 2
 Oct. 3 Royals 4 at Angels 1
 Oct. 5 Angels 3 at Royals 8

ALCS
ROYALS 4, BALTIMORE ORIOLES 0
 Oct. 10 Royals 8 at Orioles 6
 Oct. 11 Royals 6 at Orioles 4
 Oct. 14 Orioles 1 at Royals 2
 Oct. 15 Orioles 1 at Royals 2

WORLD SERIES
SAN FRANCISCO GIANTS 4, ROYALS 3
 Oct. 21 Giants 7 at Royals 1
 Oct. 22 Giants 2 at Royals 7
 Oct. 24 Royals 3 at Giants 2
 Oct. 25 Royals 4 at Giants 11
 Oct. 26 Royals 0 at Giants 5
 Oct. 28 Giants 0 at Royals 10
 Oct. 29 Giants 3 at Royals 2

It's safe to say most prognosticators did not have the Royals penciled into the 2014 postseason, let alone the World Series. After all, Kansas City owned the longest playoff drought in the Majors at the time. But the team assembled a 41-27 second-half record to clinch its first postseason berth since the city hosted a World Series champ in 1985.

After staging a dramatic rally in the eighth and ninth innings to top the

ERIC HOSMER WAS ONE OF SEVERAL ROYALS THAT SHINED IN THE FIELD THROUGHOUT THE 2014 POSTSEASON. THE FIRST BASEMAN ALSO HIT .400 IN BOTH THE ALDS AND ALCS.

A's in the Wild Card Game, the Royals swept the Angels in the ALDS. In the Championship Series, Kansas City once again made quick work of its opponent, sweeping the Orioles to clinch its first World Series berth since 1985.

In the Fall Classic, the Royals took on the San Francisco Giants, who were gunning for their third world title in five years. After falling in the opening game, Kansas City found itself tied, 2-2, more than halfway through Game 2. But the team assembled a five-run sixth inning, highlighted by Omar Infante's two-run homer, to take a 7-2 lead and win their first game of the Series. As the contest moved to San Francisco, the Royals would scratch out a one-run victory on the road to take a 2-games-to-1 Series lead. But the Giants earned a convincing 11-4 win in Game 4 to even things at a game apiece. Madison Bumgarner, who had already won a game in the Series, tossed a shutout the following night to force Kansas city to the brink of elimination.

With their backs against the wall, the Royals would respond in a big way. Behind a seven-run second-inning outburst, and Yordano Ventura's seven shutout innings, they took Game 6 in a 10-0 romp at home.

The decisive Game 7 saw the Giants jump out to a 3-2 lead in the fourth inning. In the following frame, though, Bumgarner entered in relief. The towering southpaw threw five scoreless innings to seal the victory and clinch the title for the Giants.

"These kids, from the minute you saw them, you knew they were going to be special. Their goal was to win a championship, and today they accomplished that."

Manager Ned Yost, on 2014 AL Champions

THE ROYALS WON BOTH GAMES STARTED BY VENTURA (TOP) IN THE 2014 WORLD SERIES, INCLUDING A GAME 6 ROMP IN WHICH MIKE MOUSTAKAS AND ALCIDES ESCOBAR EACH SCORED AND DROVE IN RUNS.

HOW THE ROYALS WERE BUILT

The Royals earned this crowning achievement on the strength of a roster stitched together with high draft picks and key trades. Kansas City boasted six of its own former first-round selections on its World Series roster, including stalwarts like Eric Hosmer and Alex Gordon. The squad was not complete, though, until several vital pieces from two separate blockbuster trades began to flourish. In 2010, the Royals traded their ace, Zack Greinke, to Milwaukee. In return, they received Lorenzo Cain (center field), Alcides Escobar (shortstop) and Jake Odorizzi. Two years later, Odorizzi was flipped to Tampa Bay as part of a deal that netted the Royals All-Star reliever Wade Davis.

But what separated this Kansas City team from the pack was its decision to go all-in in 2015. The small-market Royals invested in several key free agents, including Edinson Volquez and Kendrys Morales, in the offseason. Then, in the summer, the club pushed all its chips to the center of the table, acquiring All-Stars Johnny Cueto and Ben Zobrist via deadline deals. All these maneuvers resulted in a perfectly balanced roster that brought home Kansas City's first world championship in 30 years.

DRAFT

CHRISTIAN COLON	1st round, 2010
DANNY DUFFY	3rd round, 2007
JARROD DYSON	50th round, 2006
ALEX GORDON	1st round, 2005
TERRANCE GORE	1st round, 2011
GREG HOLLAND	10th round, 2007
ERIC HOSMER	1st round, 2008
MIKE MOUSTAKAS	1st round, 2007

FREE AGENCY

JOBA CHAMBERLAIN	Minor League contract (2015)
JEREMY GUTHRIE	3 years/$25.2M (2013)
KELVIN HERRERA*	2 years/$4.15M (2015)
LUKE HOCHEVAR	2 years/$10M (2015)
OMAR INFANTE	4 years/$30.25M (2014)
RYAN MADSON	1 year/$850K (2015)
KRIS MEDLEN	2 years/$8.5M (2015)
RAUL MONDESI*	Minor League contract (2011)
FRANKLIN MORALES	1 year/$1.85M (2015)
KENDRYS MORALES	2 years/$17M (2015)
SALVADOR PEREZ*	5 years/$7M (2012)
ALEX RIOS	1 year/$11M (2015)
JASON VARGAS	4 years/$32M (2014)
YORDANO VENTURA*	5 years/$23M (2015)
EDINSON VOLQUEZ	2 years/$20M (2015)
CHRIS YOUNG	1 year/$675K (2015)

Player was originally signed as an amateur free agent

TRADES

DREW BUTERA	from LAA for Ryan Jackson (2015)
LORENZO CAIN	from MIL with Alcides Escobar, Jeremy Jeffress and Jake Odorizzi for Yuniesky Betancourt, Zack Greinke and cash (2010)
JOHNNY CUETO	from CIN with cash for Cody Reed, Brandon Finnegan and John Lamb (2015)
WADE DAVIS	from TB with James Shields and Elliot Johnson for Wil Myers, Jake Odorizzi, Mike Montgomery and Patrick Leonard (2012)
ALCIDES ESCOBAR	from MIL with Lorenzo Cain, Jeremy Jeffress and Jake Odorizzi for Yuniesky Betancourt, Zack Greinke and cash (2010)
JONNY GOMES	from ATL with cash for Luis Valenzuela
PAULO ORLANDO	from CHW for Horacio Ramirez (2008)
BEN ZOBRIST	from OAK with cash for Sean Manaea and Aaron Brooks (2015)

REGULAR-SEASON RESULTS

DATE	OPP	RES	R	RA	W–L
Monday, April 6	CHW	W	10	1	1–0
Wednesday, April 8	CHW	W	7	5	2–0
Thursday, April 9	CHW	W	4	1	3–0
Friday, April 10	@LAA	W	4	2	4–0
Saturday, April 11	@LAA	W	6	4	5–0
Sunday, April 12	@LAA	W	9	2	6–0
Monday, April 13	@MIN	W	12	3	7–0
Wednesday, April 15	@MIN	L	1	3	7–1
Thursday, April 16	@MIN	L	5	8	7–2
Friday, April 17	OAK	W	6	4	8–2
Saturday, April 18	OAK	L	0	5	8–3
Sunday, April 19	OAK	W	4	2	9–3
Monday, April 20	MIN	W	7	1	10–3
Tuesday, April 21	MIN	W	6	5	11–3
Wednesday, April 22	MIN	L	0	3	11–4
Thursday, April 23	@CHW	W	3	2	12–4
Friday, April 24	@CHW	L	2	3	12–5
Sunday, April 26 (2)	@CHW	L	3	5	12–6
Monday, April 27	@CLE	W	6	2	13–6
Tuesday, April 28	@CLE	W	11	5	14–6
Wednesday, April 29	@CLE	L	5	7	14–7
Thursday, April 30	DET	W	8	1	15–7
Friday, May 1	DET	W	4	1	16–7
Saturday, May 2	DET	L	1	2	16–8
Sunday, May 3	DET	L	4	6	16–9
Tuesday, May 5	CLE	W	5	3	17–9
Wednesday, May 6	CLE	L	3	10	17–10
Thursday, May 7	CLE	W	7	4	18–10
Friday, May 8	@DET	L	5	6	18–11
Saturday, May 9	@DET	W	6	2	19–11
Sunday, May 10	@DET	W	2	1	20–11
Monday, May 11	@TEX	L	2	8	20–12
Tuesday, May 12	@TEX	W	7	6	21–12
Wednesday, May 13	@TEX	L	2	5	21–13
Thursday, May 14	@TEX	W	6	3	22–13
Friday, May 15	NYY	W	12	1	23–13
Saturday, May 16	NYY	L	1	5	23–14
Sunday, May 17	NYY	W	6	0	24–14
Tuesday, May 19	CIN	W	3	0	25–14
Wednesday, May 20	CIN	W	7	1	26–14
Friday, May 22	STL	W	5	0	27–14
Saturday, May 23	STL	W	3	2	28–14
Sunday, May 24	STL	L	1	6	28–15
Monday, May 25	@NYY	L	1	14	28–16
Tuesday, May 26	@NYY	L	1	5	28–17
Wednesday, May 27	@NYY	L	2	4	28–18
Friday, May 29	@CHC	W	8	4	29–18
Sunday, May 31	@CHC	L	1	2	29–19
Tuesday, June 2	CLE	L	1	2	29–20
Wednesday, June 3	CLE	W	4	2	30–20
Thursday, June 4	CLE	L	2	6	30–21
Friday, June 5	TEX	L	0	4	30–22
Saturday, June 6	TEX	L	2	4	30–23
Sunday, June 7	TEX	W	4	3	31–23
Monday, June 8	@MIN	W	3	1	32–23
Tuesday, June 9	@MIN	W	2	0	33–23
Wednesday, June 10	@MIN	W	7	2	34–23
Friday, June 12	@STL	L	0	4	34–24
Saturday, June 13	@STL	L	2	3	34–25
Monday, June 15	@MIL	W	8	5	35–25
Tuesday, June 16	@MIL	W	7	2	36–25
Wednesday, June 17	MIL	W	10	2	37–25
Thursday, June 18	MIL	W	3	2	38–25
Friday, June 19	BOS	L	3	7	38–26
Saturday, June 20	BOS	W	7	4	39–26
Sunday, June 21	BOS	L	2	13	39–27
Monday, June 22	@SEA	W	4	1	40–27
Tuesday, June 23	@SEA	L	0	7	40–28
Wednesday, June 24	@SEA	W	8	2	41–28
Friday, June 26	@OAK	W	5	2	42–28
Saturday, June 27	@OAK	W	3	2	43–28
Sunday, June 28	@OAK	W	5	3	44–28
Monday, June 29	@HOU	L	1	6	44–29
Tuesday, June 30	@HOU	L	0	4	44–30
Wednesday, July 1	@HOU	L	5	6	44–31
Thursday, July 2	MIN	L	0	2	44–32
Friday, July 3	MIN	W	3	2	45–32
Saturday, July 4	MIN	L	3	5	45–33
Sunday, July 5	MIN	W	3	2	46–33
Tuesday, July 7 (1)	TB	W	9	5	47–33
Tuesday, July 7 (2)	TB	W	7	1	48–33
Wednesday, July 8	TB	W	9	7	49–33

REGULAR-SEASON RESULTS

DATE	OPP	RES	R	RA	W-L
Thursday, July 9	TB	W	8	3	50-33
Friday, July 10	TOR	W	3	0	51-33
Saturday, July 11	TOR	L	2	6	51-34
Sunday, July 12	TOR	W	11	10	52-34
Friday, July 17 (1)	@CHW	W	4	2	53-34
Friday, July 17 (2)	@CHW	L	0	2	53-35
Saturday, July 18	@CHW	W	7	6	54-35
Sunday, July 19	@CHW	W	4	1	55-35
Monday, July 20	PIT	L	7	10	55-36
Tuesday, July 21	PIT	W	3	1	56-36
Wednesday, July 22	PIT	W	5	1	57-36
Thursday, July 23	@STL	L	3	4	57-37
Friday, July 24	HOU	L	0	4	57-38
Saturday, July 25	HOU	W	2	1	58-38
Sunday, July 26	HOU	W	5	1	59-38
Monday, July 27	@CLE	W	9	4	60-38
Tuesday, July 28	@CLE	W	2	1	61-38
Wednesday, July 29	@CLE	L	1	12	61-39
Thursday, July 30	@TOR	L	2	5	61-40
Friday, July 31	@TOR	L	6	7	61-41
Saturday, Aug. 1	@TOR	W	7	6	62-41
Sunday, Aug. 2	@TOR	L	2	5	62-42
Tuesday, Aug. 3	@DET	W	5	1	63-42
Wednesday, Aug. 5	@DET	L	1	2	63-43
Thursday, Aug. 6	@DET	L	6	8	63-44
Friday, Aug. 7	CHW	W	3	2	64-44
Saturday, Aug. 8	CHW	W	7	6	65-44
Sunday, Aug. 9	CHW	W	5	4	66-44
Monday, Aug. 10	DET	W	4	0	67-44
Tuesday, Aug. 11	DET	W	6	1	68-44
Wednesday, Aug. 12	DET	L	4	7	68-45
Thursday, Aug. 13	LAA	L	6	7	68-46
Friday, Aug. 14	LAA	W	4	1	69-46
Saturday, Aug. 15	LAA	W	9	4	70-46
Sunday, Aug. 16	LAA	W	4	3	71-46
Tuesday, Aug. 18	@CIN	W	3	1	72-46
Wednesday, Aug. 19	@CIN	W	4	3	73-46
Thursday, Aug. 20	@BOS	L	1	4	73-47
Friday, Aug. 21	@BOS	L	2	7	73-48
Saturday, Aug. 22	@BOS	W	6	2	74-48
Sunday, Aug. 23	@BOS	W	8	6	75-48

DATE	OPP	RES	R	RA	W-L
Monday, Aug. 24	BAL	W	8	3	76-48
Tuesday, Aug. 25	BAL	W	3	2	77-48
Wednesday, Aug. 26	BAL	L	5	8	77-49
Thursday, Aug. 27	BAL	W	5	3	78-49
Friday, Aug. 28	TB	W	3	2	79-49
Saturday, Aug. 29	TB	W	6	3	80-49
Sunday, Aug. 30	TB	L	2	3	80-50
Tuesday, Sept. 1	DET	L	5	6	80-51
Wednesday, Sept. 2	DET	W	12	1	81-51
Thursday, Sept. 3	DET	W	15	7	82-51
Friday, Sept. 4	CHW	L	1	12	82-52
Saturday, Sept. 5	CHW	L	1	6	82-53
Sunday, Sept. 6	CHW	L	5	7	82-54
Monday, Sept. 7	MIN	L	2	6	82-55
Tuesday, Sept. 8	MIN	W	4	2	83-55
Wednesday, Sept. 9	MIN	L	2	3	83-56
Friday, Sept. 11	@BAL	L	8	14	83-57
Saturday, Sept. 12	@BAL	W	14	6	84-57
Sunday, Sept. 13	@BAL	L	2	8	84-58
Monday, Sept. 14	@CLE	L	3	8	84-59
Tuesday, Sept. 15	@CLE	W	2	0	85-59
Wednesday, Sept. 16	@CLE	L	1	5	85-60
Thursday, Sept. 17	@CLE	W	8	4	86-60
Friday, Sept. 18	@DET	L	4	5	86-61
Saturday, Sept. 19	@DET	L	5	6	86-62
Sunday, Sept. 20	@DET	W	10	3	87-62
Tuesday, Sept. 22	SEA	L	2	11	87-63
Wednesday, Sept. 23	SEA	W	4	3	88-63
Thursday, Sept. 24	SEA	W	10	4	89-63
Friday, Sept. 25	CLE	L	0	6	89-64
Saturday, Sept. 26	CLE	L	5	9	89-65
Sunday, Sept. 27	CLE	W	3	0	90-65
Monday, Sept. 28	@CHC	L	0	1	90-66
Tuesday, Sept. 29	@CHW	L	2	4	90-67
Wednesday, Sept. 30	@CHW	W	5	3	91-67
Thursday, Oct. 1	@CHW	W	6	4	92-67
Friday, Oct. 2	@MIN	W	3	1	93-67
Saturday, Oct. 3	@MIN	W	5	1	94-67
Sunday, Oct. 4	@MIN	W	6	1	95-67

REGULAR-SEASON STATS

NO.	PLAYER	B/T	W	L	ERA	SO	BB	SV	BIRTHDATE	BIRTHPLACE
	PITCHERS									
62	JOBA CHAMBERLAIN	R/R	0	2	4.88	23	9	0	9/23/85	Lincoln, NE
47	JOHNNY CUETO	R/R	11	13	3.44	176	46	0	2/15/86	San Pedro de Macoris, D.R.
17	WADE DAVIS	R/R	8	1	0.94	78	20	17	9/7/85	Lake Wales, FL
41	DANNY DUFFY	L/L	7	8	4.08	102	53	1	12/21/88	Goleta, CA
11	JEREMY GUTHRIE	R/R	8	8	5.95	84	44	0	4/8/79	Roseburg, OR
40	KELVIN HERRERA	R/R	4	3	2.71	64	26	0	12/31/89	Tenares, D.R.
44	LUKE HOCHEVAR	R/R	1	1	3.73	49	16	1	9/15/83	Denver, CO
56	GREG HOLLAND	R/R	3	2	3.83	49	26	32	11/20/85	Marion, NC
46	RYAN MADSON	L/R	1	2	2.13	58	14	3	8/28/80	Long Beach, CA
39	KRIS MEDLEN	S/R	6	2	4.01	40	18	0	10/7/85	Artesia, CA
45	FRANKLIN MORALES	L/L	4	2	3.18	41	14	0	1/24/86	San Juan de los Morros, Venezuela
51	JASON VARGAS	L/L	5	2	3.98	27	12	0	2/2/83	Apple Valley, CA
30	YORDANO VENTURA	R/R	13	8	4.08	156	58	0	6/3/91	Samana, D.R.
36	EDINSON VOLQUEZ	R/R	13	9	3.55	155	72	0	7/3/83	Barahona, D.R.
32	CHRIS YOUNG	R/R	11	6	3.06	83	43	0	5/25/79	Dallas, TX

NO.	PLAYER	B/T	AB	H	AVG	HR	RBI	OBP	BIRTHDATE	BIRTHPLACE
	CATCHERS									
9	DREW BUTERA	R/R	107	21	.196	1	5	.252	8/9/83	Evansville, IN
13	SALVADOR PEREZ	R/R	531	138	.260	21	70	.280	5/10/90	Valencia, Venezuela
	INFIELDERS									
24	CHRISTIAN COLON	R/R	107	31	.290	0	6	.356	5/14/89	Cayey, Puerto Rico
2	ALCIDES ESCOBAR	R/R	612	157	.257	3	47	.293	12/16/86	La Sabana, Venezuela
35	ERIC HOSMER	L/L	599	178	.297	18	93	.363	10/24/89	South Miami, FL
14	OMAR INFANTE	R/R	440	97	.220	2	44	.234	12/26/81	Puerto la Cruz, Venezuela
21	RAUL MONDESI	S/R	0	0	.000	0	0	.000	7/27/95	Los Angeles, CA
25	KENDRYS MORALES	S/R	569	165	.290	22	106	.362	6/20/83	Fomento, Cuba
8	MIKE MOUSTAKAS	L/R	549	156	.284	22	82	.348	9/11/88	Los Angeles, CA
18	BEN ZOBRIST	S/R	467	129	.276	13	56	.359	5/26/81	Eureka, IL
	OUTFIELDERS									
6	LORENZO CAIN	R/R	551	169	.307	16	72	.361	4/13/86	Valdosta, GA
1	JARROD DYSON	L/L	200	50	.250	2	18	.311	8/15/84	McComb, MS
31	JONNY GOMES	R/R	225	48	.213	7	26	.313	11/22/80	Petaluma, CA
4	ALEX GORDON	L/R	354	96	.271	13	48	.377	2/10/84	Lincoln, NE
0	TERRANCE GORE	R/R	3	0	.000	0	0	.250	6/8/91	Macon, GA
16	PAULO ORLANDO	R/R	241	60	.249	7	27	.269	11/1/85	Sao Paulo, Brazil
15	ALEX RIOS	R/R	385	98	.255	4	32	.287	2/18/81	Coffee, AL

Manager: Ned Yost (3) **Coaches:** Dave Eiland (58), Doug Henry (57), Mike Jirschele (23), Rusty Kuntz (81), Dale Sveum (21), Don Wakamatsu (22)

THE 2015 KANSAS CITY ROYALS

NED YOST

MANAGER

The former Big League catcher has won more than 900 games as a manager, nearly 500 of which have been with the Royals. In each of the last six years, Kansas City has improved upon its record thanks to Yost's guidance, and this year the team made its second consecutive postseason appearance for the first time since 1984–85.

3

DREW BUTERA

CATCHER

After arriving in a May trade from the Angels, Butera provided a steady hand behind the plate, helping to guide a Kansas City staff that finished third in the AL in ERA.

9

LORENZO CAIN

OUTFIELD

Last year's ALCS MVP continued his dominant play in the 2015 season, posting career-high numbers in batting average, home runs, RBI and runs scored. In the decisive Game 6 of the ALCS, Cain showed off his baserunning prowess by scoring the winning run from first base on a single.

6

JOBA CHAMBERLAIN

PITCHER

Chamberlain signed with the Royals in August, providing Kansas City with another hard-throwing arm in the bullpen. The veteran reliever struck out more than 12 batters per nine innings with the club.

62

CHRISTIAN COLON

INFIELD

The 26-year-old infielder excelled against left-handed pitching in his second year with the Royals, posting a .333 batting average and .385 OBP. The Puerto Rico native also hit .414 over the last month of the regular season.

24

JOHNNY CUETO

PITCHER

Cueto proved why the Royals traded for him in July by throwing eight innings of two-run ball to secure the win in Game 5 of the ALDS and help the team advance. In Game 2 of the World Series, he became the first AL pitcher to throw a complete game in the Fall Classic since 1991.

47

WADE DAVIS

PITCHER

The All-Star reliever posted an 8-1 record with a 0.94 ERA from the 'pen this season. He assumed the closer's role late in the year and notched two saves in the ALDS. Then, in the AL Championship Series, Davis pitched a scoreless 1.2 innings in Game 6 to seal Kansas City's trip to the World Series.

17

DANNY DUFFY

PITCHER

Duffy posted a 3.62 ERA in the second half and earned his first career save on Sept. 20 after a late-season move to the 'pen. He did not allow a run in six relief appearances. The southpaw was particularly effective against left-handed hitters, posting a 3.57 K/BB ratio while holding them to a .239 average.

41

JARROD DYSON

OUTFIELD

The speedster, who manned all three outfield positions for the Royals this season, nabbed more than 20 stolen bases for the fourth consecutive year, while getting caught just three times. Dyson also tallied an additional two stolen bags in the ALDS.

1

ALCIDES ESCOBAR

SHORTSTOP

The 28-year-old collected a team-high six hits during the ALDS. He was even better in the AL Championship Series, during which he led the Royals with a .478 average en route to earning MVP honors. As an encore, he hit an inside-the-park home run in his first World Series at-bat.

2

JONNY GOMES

OUTFIELD

The veteran outfielder, acquired by the Royals on the last day of August, added a valuable weapon against left-handed pitching to the lineup. Gomes posted a .371 OBP against southpaws this season.

31

ALEX GORDON

OUTFIELD

The Gold Glove–winning outfielder did not commit an error in 2015, and returned from a serious groin injury to help the Royals down the stretch. His game-tying home run in Game 1 of the World Series off Mets closer Jeurys Familia, who up to that point had not allowed a run in the postseason, sent the game into extras before Kansas City prevailed.

TERRANCE GORE

OUTFIELD

The stolen base expert was perfect in eight steal attempts over the past two regular seasons, providing Kansas City with a late-inning threat on the base-paths. After nabbing three bags last postseason, he swiped another in this year's ALDS.

0

JEREMY GUTHRIE

PITCHER

In his fourth season with the Royals, Guthrie won seven games in the first half, tied for second most on the club, to help Kansas City race out of the gate in the AL Central.

11

KELVIN HERRERA

PITCHER

In 2015, the first-time All-Star led all Royals pitchers in appearances with 72, while holding lefties to a .151 average. He threw 5.2 scoreless innings in the ALCS, allowing just three hits and striking out 10 without issuing a walk.

40

GREG HOLLAND

PITCHER

Holland, who owns the Royals' single season record with 47 saves, notched more than 30 for the third consecutive season, despite missing the final stretch of the 2015 campaign with injury.

56

ERIC HOSMER

FIRST BASE

The former first-round pick paced all Royals batters with 178 hits and set a career high with 93 runs batted in this season. Hosmer's sixth-inning sac fly in Game 1 of the World Series gave him 24 career postseason RBI, a mark that surpassed George Brett's franchise record.

35

OMAR INFANTE

SECOND BASE

The veteran infielder, who has played almost 1,500 games in the Majors, led the Royals with seven triples in his second season with the club.

14

RYAN MADSON

PITCHER

The veteran reliever, who hadn't pitched in the Big Leagues since 2011 because of a second Tommy John surgery, dominated in his first year with the Royals. Madson posted a 2.13 ERA and 0.96 WHIP, the best marks of his career.

KRIS MEDLEN

PITCHER

Following an elbow injury that wiped out his 2014 season, Medlen posted a 6-2 record while splitting time between the 'pen and the starting rotation. In 30 innings of work on the road, he pitched to a 1.20 ERA.

39

RAUL MONDESI

INFIELD

Mondesi, rated the Royals' No. 1 prospect by MLB.com, received his first Big League call-up just before the World Series began, adding speed and a steady infield glove to Kansas City's roster. The polished defender tallied five triples and 19 stolen bases in Double-A this season.

27

FRANKLIN MORALES

PITCHER

The nine-year veteran recorded his lowest career marks in ERA and WHIP this season while holding lefties to a minuscule .192 batting average.

47

KENDRYS MORALES

DESIGNATED HITTER

After tying for the club lead in homers during a resurgent regular season, Morales belted a team-high three longballs in the ALDS. He also tallied 106 RBI during the 2015 campaign, his highest total in six years.

25

MIKE MOUSTAKAS

THIRD BASE

Moustakas, a first-time All-Star in 2015, drilled a team- and career-high 22 regular-season homers alongside career-best marks in batting average, RBI and runs scored. The Royals' 2007 first-round pick, who belted five longballs during the 2014 postseason, went deep in this year's Game 6 ALCS win.

8

THE 2015 KANSAS CITY ROYALS

PAULO ORLANDO

OUTFIELD

The rookie legged out three straight triples for his first three career hits and heated up down the stretch, batting .311 from Sept. 1 through the end of the regular season.

16

SALVADOR PEREZ

CATCHER

The 2015 World Series MVP led all AL catchers in hits for the third consecutive season and launched two home runs in Kansas City's ALDS triumph over the Astros. The backstop tied a team high with four home runs through the first two rounds of the postseason.

13

THE 2015 KANSAS CITY ROYALS

ALEX RIOS

OUTFIELD

Rios provided a veteran presence in the Royals' outfield and showed his mettle with a go-ahead, two-run double in Game 5 of the ALDS. He was even better in the AL Championship Series, during which he batted .368 over the six games.

15

JASON VARGAS

PITCHER

In his second season with the Royals, the veteran Vargas won five of his seven decisions before missing the remainder of the year with an elbow injury.

51

YORDANO VENTURA

PITCHER

The 24-year-old fireballer led the Royals in strikeouts and tied for the team-high mark with 13 wins. Ventura went 8-1 over the final two months of the regular season before starting four games in the first two rounds of the postseason, all but one of which resulted in a Royals win.

30

EDINSON VOLQUEZ

PITCHER

In his first year with the Royals, Volquez was a workhorse, leading the team in starts and throwing more than 200 innings for the first time in his career. In Game 1 of the ALCS, the right-hander tossed six scoreless innings to earn his first career postseason win.

CHRIS YOUNG

PITCHER

Young held opponents to a .202 average in 34 appearances this year, and was just as effective out of the 'pen as he was in the rotation. He started and helped pitch the Royals to a Game 4 victory in the ALCS before tallying another win in extras during Game 1 of the Fall Classic.

32

BEN ZOBRIST

SECOND BASE

Zobrist shored up Kansas City's infield after arriving via a July trade. He only improved in the playoffs, the first two rounds of which he posted a .326 average and scored a team-high 10 runs.

18

CENTER STAGE

Humble and graceful behind the scenes, acrobatic Royals center fielder Lorenzo Cain turns up the volume in the spotlight.

When the Royals burst onto the national stage last October, fans everywhere got perhaps their first extended look at the fun-loving, fearless, wall-crashing style of play of Lorenzo Cain. Royals fans had seen Cain patrol the outfield with reckless abandon for years. Now it was the nation's turn to fall in love with his speed, grace and, of course, that electric smile. A Gold Glove candidate in center, Cain put on an amazing display during the 2014 postseason with an array of diving grabs in the alleys and body-bruising catches against the fences. A popular tweet at the time reprised an old quote about Phillies outfielder Garry Maddox: "Water covers 72 percent of the Earth. Lorenzo Cain covers the rest."

But beyond his fascinating athleticism, Cain's popularity among fans stems from his seemingly boundless love for the game. "You can always tell he's having a good time," teammate Eric Hosmer says. "He loves to play."

As the Royals headed into the playoffs for the second consecutive season, the 2014 ALCS MVP and first-time All-Star in '15 gave MLB some insight into the inner-workings of a burgeoning star.

Last October was so crazy. How long did it take you to put everything in perspective?
Once I got into the offseason, it was still a little painful. Afterward, I watched a lot of the games online. I definitely appreciate how far we made it and how hard we fought as a team to get a chance to go to the World Series. Unfortunately we lost, but the experience was once-in-a lifetime.

Did it make you hungrier to go back and win it all?
Most definitely. Coming into this season, a lot of people didn't expect us to keep winning; they called last year a fluke. We just set out to prove people wrong, and we've definitely done that. Our main goal was to get back to the postseason.

Do you have a favorite memory from the 2014 World Series?
I can't pick just one. I have a lot of memories, from the way we came back in the Wild Card Game to all the catches and plays we made as a team, and all the clutch hits that guys came up with.

Was your first World Series purely a fun experience, or did you feel any pressure?
I don't think there was pressure, even though it was our first time. For a group of guys getting a chance to play in the postseason or the World Series for the first time, I don't think we were nervous. It was all adrenaline; we were fired up and hungry. We wanted to bring a championship to the city. I felt like we did a great job of coming together and playing as a team. I definitely enjoyed the entire experience.

Young fans idolize you, largely because of your style of play. How does that make you feel?
A lot of moms and dads come up to me and tell me they appreciate the way I go about the game. They're always telling me that their little kids are getting into baseball now, too. That puts a smile on my face. I just try to go out there and get it done on the field and be the playmaker I know I can be.

If you were a young fan, would you enjoy watching yourself play?
I think I would, especially with all of my diving catches in the postseason. I don't think I've ever had that many opportunities to make diving or sliding catches before. They came one after another, and fortunately I was able to make them all. It was definitely a nice feeling and it came at the right moment on baseball's biggest stage.

You never played Little League Baseball as a kid. Do you think you missed out?
I understand the situation with my single mom; it would have been an extra burden on her. I decided not to worry her with it. I just helped around the house. Once things got a little easier and I was in high school, that's when I took full advantage and tried to play this game I love. I'm glad I got the chance to make the most out of it and get to the World Series. It's definitely been a thrill ride for me.

Rumor has it that you got cut from your high school basketball team. Tell us about that experience.
(Leans back and laughs) I definitely wasn't expecting it. It hurt when I didn't see my name on the list. Everything works out for a reason, though; if I had made the team, I would never have tried out for baseball. It has been a long journey, and it hasn't been easy. There have been a lot of ups and downs, but I have a great support system that has pushed me and motivated me to the fullest. Now I'm here on a Big League team. It was definitely worth the wait.

Your high school coach said he was 90 percent sure that you had never played, and maybe never even seen, a baseball game before you tried out.
(Laughs) I had never watched baseball. My mom wouldn't let me play football and now you know the story about me getting cut from the basketball team, so all that was left at my small high school was baseball. I had a buddy who played, and I asked him if there was any way I could make the team. They actually needed an extra guy on the JV squad, so it all worked out. I was kind of the savior of the season.

Is it true that you didn't even own a glove back then?
I did not. When I made the team I had to borrow everything: bat, glove, batting gloves, cleats. You name it, I borrowed it. It was difficult at first, but I had a lot of great friends on the team. And my coach took me home each and every day. A lot of people helped me along the way, I will say that.

Your mom, Patricia, taught you to be a humble guy. Is it hard to show humility after winning an ALCS MVP Award and playing in the World Series?
I don't think so. It's all about how you grew up and where you came from. A lot of people may put you on a pedestal, but I just go about it day by day and understand that it's work. I try to have a good time.

Your best friend, Jeremy Haynes, told me that your diet in college consisted of cookies & cream ice cream and Coco Puffs. True story?
Very true. I'm addicted to those foods and still eat them to this day. In college you're on a small budget, so it's ramen noodles, ice cream and cereal.

When it comes to music, you're an old-school guy. How did "Trap Queen" by Fetty Wap become your walk-up song?
I've got to mix it up now and then. Like you said, I am old-school: Jackson 5, Marvin Gaye, Satchmo, Temptations. [Trap Queen] is just the new-school.

Last year, the team thrived on Archie Eversole's "We Ready." This year it's "Trap Queen." Is there going to be a theme song every season?
As long as this group is together. It's a tight group, and we try to find ways to have fun. I know we're not going to play together forever, so we just try to enjoy every moment and have fun. Right now we're just enjoying this run and making it last as long as we can.

THE ROYAL CROWN

The 2015 Royals provided a fitting recent example of just how quickly the baseball world can be turned upside down. Entering last season, the club possessed the longest postseason drought in the Majors. Kansas City erased that distinction with a memorable run to the World Series last year and followed it up with a dominant 2015 campaign, punctuated by the AL's best record. After another dramatic and hard-fought pennant win, the Royals returned to the Fall Classic and did what they couldn't the year before: win it all.

THE ROYALS OPENED THE 2015
SEASON AT KAUFFMAN
STADIUM BOASTING A ROSTER
FILLED WITH PLAYERS
SEEKING A RETURN TRIP TO
THE FALL CLASSIC.

THE ROYALS' ROCK SOLID DEFENSE HAS BEEN A LARGE REASON FOR THE TEAM'S SUCCESS. LEFT FIELDER ALEX GORDON HAS WON MULTIPLE GOLD GLOVE AWARDS IN HIS NINE-YEAR TENURE, WHILE SURE-HANDED SHORTSTOP ALCIDES ESCOBAR (TOP) SHORES UP THE INFIELD.

YOUNG STARS ERIC
HOSMER (CLOCKWISE FROM
TOP LEFT) AND SALVADOR
PEREZ WERE BOTH SIGNED
AND DEVELOPED BY THE
ROYALS ORGANIZATION,
WHILE LORENZO CAIN HAS
SPENT ALL BUT ONE
SEASON OF HIS CAREER
WITH THE CLUB.

GATORADE SHOWERS WERE
A COMMON OCCURRENCE
FOR THE ROYALS, AS THEY
CELEBRATED AN AMERICAN
LEAGUE–BEST 95 WINS
THIS SEASON, MORE THAN
HALF OF WHICH CAME IN
FRONT OF THE KAUFFMAN
STADIUM FAITHFUL.

MIKE MOUSTAKAS AND
HOSMER CELEBRATED THE
ROYALS' AL CENTRAL
TITLE IN SEPTEMBER.
AFTER FIGHTING JUST TO
EARN A WILD CARD BERTH
LAST YEAR, KANSAS CITY
LED ITS DIVISION
WIRE-TO-WIRE IN 2015.

KANSAS CITY ROYALS
2015 MINOR LEAGUE RESULTS

AAA OMAHA STORM CHASERS (80-64)
Tied for 2nd in Pacific Coast League American Northern Division

AA NORTHWEST ARKANSAS NATURALS (69-70)
2nd in Texas League North Division

HIGH-A WILMINGTON BLUE ROCKS (62-77)
4th in Carolina League Northern Division

CLASS-A LEXINGTON LEGENDS (58-80)
6th in South Atlantic League Southern Division

ROOKIE IDAHO FALLS CHUKARS (38-38)
3rd in Pioneer League South Division

ROOKIE BURLINGTON ROYALS (31-37)
4th in Appalachian League East Division

ARIZONA LEAGUE ROYALS (40-16)
1st in Arizona League West Division

A DECADE OF CHAMPIONS

Unprecedented parity during the latest era of Major League Baseball has ushered 12 different ballclubs into the World Series in the past decade. Of those teams, six have come out on top.

2005

CHICAGO WHITE SOX

One decade ago, the White Sox ended an 87-year drought when they swept the Astros in the 2005 World Series. Chicago had finished with the best record in the American League, while Houston claimed a Wild Card berth on the way to the franchise's first-ever World Series.

Billed as a clash between two fearsome pitching staffs, the contest began as anything but. Astros ace Roger Clemens left Game 1 early with a sore hamstring, while Jose Contreras allowed three runs but still secured the win for the South Siders. In Game 2, Houston got to Sox ace Mark Buehrle, but Scott Podsednik kept Chicago alive with a game-winning blast. Game 3 was a marathon, as the teams combined to employ a Series-record 43 players in 14 innings. The Sox ultimately prevailed, 7–5.

A pitchers' duel finally arrived in Game 4, as Freddy Garcia and Brandon Backe kept things scoreless until the eighth. Eventual Series MVP Jermaine Dye hit a go-ahead single, though, and the 1–0 margin was enough for the White Sox to complete the sweep.

CLOSER BOBBY JENKS AND CATCHER A.J. PIERZYNSKI CELEBRATED THE FINAL OUT OF THE WHITE SOX'S GAME 4 VICTORY, WHICH CLINCHED THE FRANCHISE'S FIRST CHAMPIONSHIP IN NEARLY A CENTURY.

ECKSTEIN TOOK HOME WORLD SERIES MVP HONORS AFTER BATTING .364 IN THE CARDINALS' FIVE-GAME SERIES WIN OVER THE TIGERS.

2006

ST. LOUIS CARDINALS

From 2000–05, the Cardinals had reached the playoffs in all but one year, advanced to the NLCS three times, and competed for one World Series title. But until 2006, they hadn't actually won it all since way back in 1982.

Despite finishing with nearly 20 fewer regular-season victories than they had in the previous two seasons (the club went 105-57 in 2004 and 100-62 in '05), the Cardinals put it all together against Detroit in 2006. Twice in the five-game Series, St. Louis defeated the Tigers' Justin Verlander, including in Game 1, when the visiting club sent Verlander to the showers after he surrendered six runs in five innings. Albert Pujols and Scott Rolen each contributed to the Cardinals' offensive onslaught, slugging a home run apiece.

Although St. Louis would not go yard for the rest of the Series, the entire lineup played a role in the victory. In fact, light-hitting infielder David Eckstein, who helped the Angels to a title four years prior, proved to be the star, earning Series MVP honors on the heels of an eight-hit, three-run, four-RBI performance. Detroit showed some life at home in Game 2, which they won, 3-1, but the Cardinals ultimately outscored the Tigers, 22-11, over the course of the Series to clinch their first title in more than two decades at Busch Stadium.

WORLD SERIES MVP LOWELL BATTED .400 WITH A HOME RUN AND FOUR RBI IN BOSTON'S FOUR-GAME SWEEP OF COLORADO. IT WAS THE RED SOX'S SECOND CHAMPIONSHIP IN FOUR SEASONS FOLLOWING AN 86-YEAR TITLE DROUGHT.

> *"When you play in the World Series, someone has to go home."*
>
> *Phillies Manager Charlie Manuel*

2007

BOSTON RED SOX

Some moments in time, although it may not be obvious as they happen, can carry great symbolic weight. In 2007, the Red Sox's Mike Lowell had enjoyed one of his most successful campaigns. What best served to endear him to fans forever, though, was a magnificent performance in that year's World Series.

Lowell, who in 1999 had battled testicular cancer as a member of the Marlins, willed the Red Sox's offense to overcome the Colorado Rockies and finish off a Series sweep. Boston's bats chased Rockies starting pitcher Jeff Francis early in Game 1 while romping to a 13-1 victory. Game 2 was a tighter, 2-1 affair, but the Sox still prevailed at home. When the Series flipped to Coors Field, the visitors rolled again, taking a commanding 3-games-to-none lead.

In the seventh inning of Game 4, Lowell padded the Sox's lead with a solo home run off Aaron Cook. The World Series MVP Award winner's blast proved to be the difference-maker.

Hitting fifth in the lineup behind formidable sluggers Manny Ramirez and David Ortiz, it was Lowell who provided most of the offensive thunder throughout the Fall Classic, batting .400 with four extra-base hits — and adding a stolen base for good measure — as Beantown celebrated its second world title in four years.

2008

PHILADELPHIA PHILLIES

The 2008 Series was a study in contrasts. While the Phillies' front office proved it was willing to invest heavily in the future, the Rays epitomized a small-market club. Philadelphia had history and a World Series title under its belt; Tampa Bay, meanwhile, had never finished better than fourth place in the AL East, and that happened only once in its first decade of existence. And as comfortable as the mid-70-degree nights were when the Series opened at Tropicana Field, things were equally miserable at Citizens Bank Park, as temperatures plunged to the mid-40s and monsoon-like conditions postponed play. At one point, Commissioner Bud Selig even declared, "We'll celebrate [Thanksgiving] here if we have to."

Thankfully, it didn't quite come to that. Instead, 2006 National League MVP Ryan Howard knocked three homers for the victorious club, while veterans Jimmy Rollins, Carlos Ruiz, Shane Victorino and Jayson Werth joined him to provide all the pop the offense needed to stay on top. The Phillies' bats were especially potent in Game 4, knocking 10 runs against a foursome of Rays pitchers.

Philadelphia's staff, on the other hand, featured farm system product Cole Hamels, who combined with Joe Blanton and J.C. Romero to collect all four Fall Classic wins while limiting the Rays to just one. When closer Brad Lidge locked down his second save in the clinching Game 5, he brought fans along with him to their knees.

LIDGE CELEBRATED WITH RUIZ ON THE FIELD AT CITIZENS BANK PARK AFTER NOTCHING THE SAVE IN THE DECIDING GAME 5 OF THE '08 WORLD SERIES.

A DECADE OF CHAMPIONS

2009

NEW YORK YANKEES

It was a bold move when new Yankees Manager Joe Girardi donned a No. 27 jersey at the 2007 press conference announcing his hiring. But everyone knew its significance. So it was especially sweet when the man wearing No. 27 joined his charges in celebrating the team's 27th championship just two years later.

The 2009 Yankees were champions because their core of veterans — Derek Jeter, Mariano Rivera, Jorge Posada and Andy Pettitte — meshed perfectly with the reinforcements brought in by GM Brian Cashman and his staff. Pettitte notched two wins and Rivera a pair of saves in the World Series alone. Alex Rodriguez launched six home runs that October. And Series MVP Hideki Matsui posted an otherworldly 2.027 OPS in 13 Fall Classic at-bats.

Those performances helped the Yankees outlast a Phillies team gunning for a dramatic repeat. Despite a historic hitting display by Chase Utley, untouchable curveballs from Cliff Lee and the confidence of having been there a year earlier, the Phillies dropped three straight after winning Game 1, and didn't recover. After sending the Series back to the Bronx for Game 6, Philadelphians could only watch as Godzilla (as Matsui was affectionately called) trampled their city's title hopes.

"When you play in the World Series, someone has to go home," Phillies Manager Charlie Manuel said after Game 6. "All of a sudden you play four out of seven and then lose, and someone tells you to go home."

In the end, it was New York's year. For the 27th time, the Yankees were world champs.

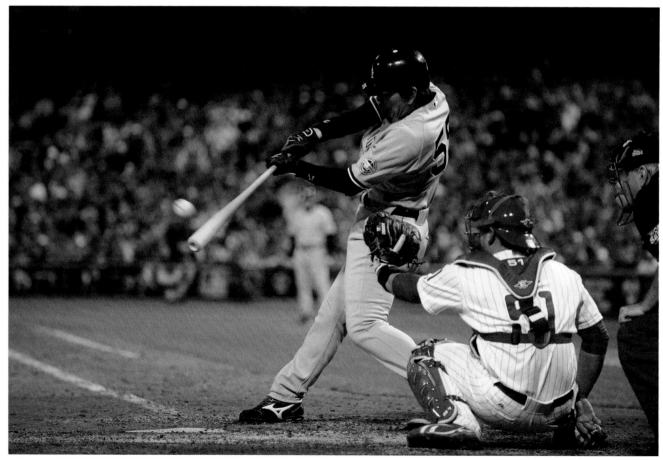

MATSUI POSTED AN INCREDIBLE .615 BATTING AVERAGE AGAINST THE PHILLIES IN THE '09 WORLD SERIES, INCLUDING A 3-FOR-4, SIX-RBI PERFORMANCE IN THE DECISIVE GAME 6.

AFTER EARNING A WIN IN EACH OF THE FIRST TWO ROUNDS OF THE POSTSEASON, LINCECUM WON A PAIR OF GAMES IN THE FALL CLASSIC, INCLUDING A DOMINANT EIGHT-INNING START IN THE DECISIVE GAME 5.

2010

SAN FRANCISCO GIANTS

Going into the 2010 postseason, it seemed that most of the media's attention was directed away from the dominant staff in San Francisco, led by Tim Lincecum. Instead, the focus was locked on the Phillies' rotation and the Rangers' potent offense. Throughout that postseason, though, the 2008 NL Cy Young Award winner made sure that neither he, nor the rest of the Giants rotation, would be overlooked again.

Lincecum dominated in his first career playoff start with one of the best games of his already impressive career. He struck out an incredible 14 Braves while allowing just two hits. Lincecum then set the tone in the NLCS by beating the Phillies in Game 1, outdueling ace Roy Halladay and striking out eight.

And Lincecum was just as dominant in the World Series, where he matched up with Rangers ace Cliff Lee, who through that point was 7-0 in the postseason with a microscopic 1.26 ERA. To the delight of fans, the right-hander would face off against Lee a second time in the Series, as well. Lincecum got the better of him in both outings, winning Game 1 and then shoring up the Giants' World Series victory with eight stellar innings in Game 5 to wrap up one of the most overpowering October pitching performances in baseball history.

IN HIS LAST SEASON AT THE HELM OF THE CARDINALS, LA RUSSA WILLED HIS CLUB INTO THE POSTSEASON. FROM THERE, ST. LOUIS PULLED OFF A DRAMATIC OCTOBER RUN, CULMINATING IN A GAME 7 WORLD SERIES WIN.

2011

ST. LOUIS CARDINALS

On Aug. 25, 2011, the Cardinals were nine-and-a-half games behind the first-place Milwaukee Brewers in the NL Central. With five weeks left in the season, their playoff hopes were slim.

At that point, Cardinals Manager Tony La Russa, who was set to retire after the season, gathered his troops. "Play every game like it's the last game of your life," he urged. The mantra worked, as the Cards would finish on a 22-9 run, narrowly securing the Wild Card spot.

After fashioning that comeback, the Cardinals would just keep coming back. They came from behind to top the Phillies in the Division Series before repeating the feat against the Brewers in the NLCS. In Game 6 of the World Series, the Cards trailed the Rangers, 3 games to 2, when NLCS and eventual Series MVP David Freese came to the plate in the ninth with two on and two outs. He tripled in both runners, knotting the score and sending the game to extras. Leading off the 11th, Freese came through with the game-winning home run. St. Louis took Game 7, too, after the third baseman hit a two-run double in the first inning.

"It was overwhelming," said La Russa. "We were on the edge game after game after game. [When] you play with that urgency, it's a little scary at times, but it's really fun to compete that way."

> "We were on the edge game after game after game. When you play with that urgency, it's a little scary at times, but it's really fun to compete that way."
>
> *Cardinals Manager Tony La Russa*

2012

SAN FRANCISCO GIANTS

In 2012, the Giants were just two years removed from their 2010 title, and two regular-season wins better than that year's postseason contenders. But they were also just one year removed from a season in which they finished eight games out of the playoffs, and needed to neutralize the Tigers and ace Justin Verlander if they were again to achieve glory.

Pablo Sandoval dominated the opening game with a record-tying three-longball performance. Game 2 remained scoreless for several frames, as starters Madison Bumgarner and Doug Fister traded zeroes through six-and-a-half. But the Giants eventually eked out two runs, and Sergio Romo preserved the victory with a perfect ninth inning. Detroit was again unable to score in Game 3, this time against Ryan Vogelsong, who just two years before had been released from a Minor League contract.

The fearless team sent ace Matt Cain to the hill for Game 4, and jumped on the scoreboard in the second inning. The Tigers roared back, however, when Miguel Cabrera launched a two-run shot to give them their first lead of the entire Series. But the Giants, too, had an MVP candidate in the lineup, and Buster Posey belted a two-run homer of his own to regain the lead for the Giants, 3-2.

A Delmon Young longball in the bottom of the sixth tied the score again, but NLCS hero Marco Scutaro again came through with a two-out RBI single in extra innings that proved to be the game, and Series, winner.

SANDOVAL WENT DEEP THREE TIMES IN A RECORD-TYING PERFORMANCE IN GAME 1, HELPING TO LEAD THE GIANTS TO THEIR SECOND TITLE IN THREE YEARS.

UEHARA JUMPED INTO THE ARMS OF DAVID ROSS AFTER RECORDING THE LAST OUT OF THE 2013 WORLD SERIES. BOSTON'S THIRD TITLE IN A DECADE WAS THE FIRST CLINCHED AT FENWAY PARK IN ALMOST 100 YEARS.

2013

BOSTON RED SOX

After finishing last in the American League East in 2012 with a 69–93 record, the Boston Red Sox were faced with the formidable challenge of regaining respect in 2013. Under new skipper John Farrell, they managed to reverse course, finishing with an AL-best 97–65 record. The St. Louis Cardinals, meanwhile, came just one victory shy of the World Series in 2012, losing to the eventual champion San Francisco Giants.

When the teams met in the 2013 Classic, Boston got off to a quick start, scoring five runs in the first two innings off Cards ace Adam Wainwright, leading to an 8–1 win. St. Louis bounced back to capture Games 2 and 3, the latter on an obstruction call, which marked the first time a World Series game ended on such a play. In the bottom of the ninth, with the score level at 4–4, Allen Craig scored the game-winning run after tripping over third baseman Will Middlebrooks.

The Red Sox rebounded to win the next two games before going up against Michael Wacha, who had previously been unbeaten in the playoffs, at the Fens for Game 6. Boston scored three runs each in the third and fourth innings, and when Koji Uehara struck out Matt Carpenter to end the game, it sealed the Red Sox's third championship in 10 years and the first title at Fenway Park since 1918.

2014

SAN FRANCISCO GIANTS

The 2014 Fall Classic featured two teams with drastically different recent postseason histories. The Kansas City Royals hadn't played October baseball since they won it all in 1985. The San Francisco Giants, meanwhile, were gunning for their third world title in five years, and they would earn that crown thanks to a legendary performance from starting pitcher Madison Bumgarner.

After securing a dominant, 7–1 win in the opener at Kansas City's Kauffman Stadium, Bumgarner returned to the mound again for Game 5 at AT&T Park, where he tossed a shutout in front of a hometown crowd to help the Giants regain the Series advantage. But following a 10–0, Game 6 loss in which San Francisco's bats went silent, Bumgarner stepped up in a big way. The towering southpaw threw five innings of scoreless relief in Game 7 to earn the save and clinch the franchise's eighth World Series title.

"[Bumgarner] is a guy that is able to elevate his game," Buster Posey said. "He's extremely competitive."

The southpaw allowed just one run over 21 innings en route to being named the Series MVP. In the process, he lowered his career Fall Classic ERA to 0.25, the best all-time among pitchers with at least 20 World Series innings pitched.

> **"[Bumgarner] is a guy that is able to elevate his game. He's extremely competitive."**
>
> *Buster Posey*

IN ONE OF THE GREATEST PITCHING PERFORMANCES IN WORLD SERIES HISTORY, BUMGARNER WON TWO GAMES AND PICKED UP A FIVE-INNING SAVE IN THE CLINCHING GAME 7. THE TOWERING SOUTHPAW LOWERED HIS CAREER FALL CLASSIC ERA TO A RECORD 0.25.

MAJOR LEAGUE BASEBALL

President, Business & Media	Bob Bowman
Executive Vice President, Content; Editor-in-Chief, MLBAM	Dinn Mann
Vice President, Publishing	Donald S. Hintze
Editorial Director	Mike McCormick
Publications Art Director	Faith M. Rittenberg
Senior Production Manager	Claire Walsh
Account Executive	Jake Schwartzstein
Associate Editor	Allison Duffy
Specialist, Content Media	Alex Trautwig
Project Designer	Melanie Finnern
Project Assistant Editors	Andrew Sheldon, Joe Sparacio

MAJOR LEAGUE BASEBALL PHOTOS

Manager	Jessica Carroll
Photo Editor	Jim McKenna

WORLD SERIES CONTRIBUTING PHOTOGRAPHERS

Brad Mangin, LG Patterson, Rob Tringali, Ron Vesely

FENN M&S

THE FENN / McCLELLAND & STEWART TEAM

President & CEO	Brad Martin
President & Publisher, PRHC	Kristin Cochrane
Publisher, FENN	C. Jordan Fenn
Executive Managing Editor	Elizabeth Kribs
EVP, Director of Production	Janine Laporte
Senior Production Coordinator	Christie Hanson
EVP, Director of Sales	Duncan Shields
VP, Director of Sales	James Young
Publicity Manager	Ruta Liormonas
Senior Marketing Director	Constance Mackenzie
Typesetter	Erin Cooper
Designer	Five Seventeen

PHOTO CREDITS

Justin K. Aller/Getty Images: 29 (Cole)

Taylor Baucom/MLB Photos: 32

Al Bello/Getty Images: 31 (Scherzer, Yankees), 136

Jon Blacker/MLB Photos: 52, 53 (Morales), 58 (Estrada)

Rob Carr/Getty Images: 49, 50, 51 (Tulowitzki), 65

Anthony Causi/MLB Photos: 22, 33 (Price), 120 (Guthrie)

Rey Del Rio/MLB Photos: 21 (Price)

Jon Durr/Getty Images: 23 (Bryant), 108

Dave Einsel/MLB Photos: 33 (Keuchel), 38, 39

Rich Gagnon/Getty Images: 27 (Ortiz), 135

Barry Gossage/MLB Photos: 33 (Greinke)

Reed Hoffmann/Getty Images: 110

Harry How/Getty Images: 31 (Arenado), 56, 57 (Hochevar), 58 (Colabello), 129

Rob Leiter/MLB Photos: 33 (Kershaw)

Bob Levey/Getty Images: 21 (Trout), 40

Brad Mangin/MLB Photos: 10 (fans), 11 (Cueto), 14, 15, 67, 75 (Moustakas, Zobrist), 80 (Syndergaard), 81 (Rios), 87 (Davis), 90, 93 (Hosmer), 157, 158

Jim McIsaac/Getty Images: 35 (Matz)

Jason Miller/Getty Images: 126 (Medlen)

MLB Photos: 101

NBLA/MLB Photos: 98, 99

LG Patterson/MLB Photos: Back cover (Cain), 9 (3), 11 (postgame), 12 (Gordon, Rios), 16, 17, 26, 27 (Frazier), 34, 35, 44, 45 (2), 46, 47, 61, 64 (Escobar), 68 (dugout), 81 (stands), 84, 87 (Perez), 93, 97, 122, 139, 141, 144 (Escobar)

Dave Reginek/Getty Images: 121

Vaughn Ridley/Getty Images: 55

Jim Rogash/Getty Images: 23 (Rodriguez), 25 (Venditte, 2)

Joe Skipper/Getty Images: 29 (Gordon)

Eric Christian Smith/Getty Images: 41

Jamie Squire/Getty Images: 21 (Orlando), 28, 30, 36, 37 (Hosmer), 51 (Zobrist), 60, 62, 63 (2), 64 (Ventura), 109, 113, 118, 119, 120 (Gore), 131, 133, 134, 137, 146

Mike Stobe/Getty Images: 27 (Greinke)

Amy Stroth/MLB Photos: 102

Tom Szczerbowski/Getty Images: 25 (Fielder), 29 (Hawkins), 53 (Tulowitzki), 54, 57 (Zobrist), 59

Alex Trautwig/MLB Photos: 19

Rob Tringali/MLB Photos: Front cover, 7, 10 (Zobrist, Perez), 20, 66, 68 (Gordon), 73, 74, 76, 80 (stadium), 82, 88, 91, 92, 103 (2), 144 (Gordon), 159

Rich Pilling/MLB Photos: 150, 153, 154, 156

Ron Vesely/MLB Photos: 8 (3), 11 (Moustakas), 12 (team), 13 (all), 68 (Harvey), 69, 70, 75 (Hosmer), 78, 79, 81 (Zobrist, Hochevar), 85, 86 (stadium, Moustakas), 87 (Rios), 93 (Cain), 94, 151, 152, 155

Dilip Vishwanat/Getty Images: 23 (Holliday)

John Williamson/MLB Photos: 17, 24, 97, 112 (Colon), 115, 116 (2), 117, 123, 124, 125, 126 (Morales), 127, 130, 145 (Perez)

Ed Zurga/Getty Images: Back cover (Morales, Moustakas), 37 (Zobrist), 42, 43, 48, 112 (Chamberlain), 132, 143, 145 (Hosmer, Cain), 147 (3), 148

ISBN: 978-0-7710-5976-6
Library and Archives Canada Cataloguing in Publication is available upon request

Published simultaneously in the United States of America by Fenn/McClelland & Stewart, a division of Random House of Canada Limited, a Penguin Random House Company.

Library of Congress Control Number is available upon request

Printed and bound in the United States of America

McClelland & Stewart,
a division of Random House of Canada Limited,
a Penguin Random House Company
www.penguinrandomhouse.ca

1   2   3   4   5   18   17   16   15

FENN
M&S

CONTENTS